access to history

The PEOPLE'S REPUBLIC OF CHINA *since 1949*

Michael Lynch

cirencester college

HODDER HEADLINE GROUP

Orders: please contact Bookpoint Ltd, 130 Milton Park Abingdon, Oxon OX14 4SB. Telephone: (44) 01235 827720, Fax: (44) 01235 400454. Lines are open from 9.00–6.00, Monday to Saturday, with a 24 hour message answering service. You can also order through our website at www.hodderheadline.co.uk

British Library Cataloguing in Publication Data

A catalogue for this title is available from the British Library

ISBN 0 340 68853 X

First published 1998

Impression number	10	9	8	7	6
Year	2004	2003			

Cover photo courtesy of Camera Press

Illustrations by Ian Foulis & Associates Ltd, Plymouth
Typeset by Sempringham publishing services, Bedford
Printed in Great Britain for Hodder & Stoughton Educational,
a division of Hodder Headline, 338 Euston Road, London NW1 3BH
by The Bath Press, Bath

Contents

Note on spellings

There are two main styles of transliterating Chinese names into English, the older Wade-Giles system and the more recent Pinyin form. In this book it is Pinyin that is normally used. To avoid confusion, the Wade-Giles or alternative form is added in brackets after the first appearance of the name. There is also a glossary at the back of the book, giving a list of names in both forms.

Preface

To the general reader

Although the *Access to History* series has been designed with the needs of students studying the subject at higher examination levels very much in mind, it also has a great deal to offer the general reader. The main body of the text (i.e. ignoring the 'Study Guides' at the ends of chapters) forms a readable and yet stimulating survey of a coherent topic as studied by historians. However, each author's aim has not merely been to provide a clear explanation of what happened in the past (to interest and inform): it has also been assumed that most readers wish to be stimulated into thinking further about the topic and to form opinions of their own about the significance of the events that are described and discussed (to be challenged). Thus, although no prior knowledge of the topic is expected on the reader's part, she or he is treated as an intelligent and thinking person throughout. The author tends to share ideas and possibilities with the reader, rather than passing on numbers of so-called 'historical truths'.

To the student reader

There are many ways in which the series can be used by students studying history at a higher level. It will, therefore, be worthwhile thinking about your own study strategy before you start your work on this book. Obviously, your strategy will vary depending on the aim you have in mind, and the time for study that is available to you.

If, for example, you want to acquire a general overview of the topic in the shortest possible time, the following approach will probably be the most effective:

1. Read Chapter 1 and think about its contents.
2. Read the 'Making notes' section at the end of Chapter 2 and decide whether it is necessary for you to read this chapter.
3. If it is, read the chapter, stopping at each heading to note down the main points that have been made.
4. Repeat stage 2 (and stage 3 where appropriate) for all the other chapters.

If, however, your aim is to gain a thorough grasp of the topic, taking however much time is necessary to do so, you may benefit from carrying out the same procedure with each chapter, as follows:

1. Read the chapter as fast as you can, and preferably at one sitting.
2. Study the flow diagram at the end of the chapter, ensuring that you understand the general 'shape' of what you have just read.

3. Read the 'Making notes' section (and the 'Answering essay questions' section, if there is one) and decide what further work you need to do on the chapter. In particularly important sections of the book, this will involve reading the chapter a second time and stopping at each heading to think about (and to write a summary of) what you have just read.
4. Attempt the 'Source-based questions' section. It will sometimes be sufficient to think through your answers, but additional understanding will often be gained by forcing yourself to write them down.

When you have finished the main chapters of the book, study the 'Further Reading' section and decide what additional reading (if any) you will do on the topic.

   This book has been designed to help make your studies both enjoyable and successful. If you can think of ways in which this could have been done more effectively, please write to tell me. In the meantime, I hope that you will gain greatly from your study of History.

Keith Randell

Acknowledgements

The Publishers would like to thank the following for permission to reproduce the following material:

The BBC World Service for extracts taken from the transcript of a BBC World Service programme entitled *The Cultural Revolution* which was broadcast in July, 1996; Van Nostrand for the extract from *The Road to Communism: China since 1912* by Dun J. Li (Ed) (1969); WW Norton for an extract from *The Search for Modern China* by Jonathan D. Spence (1990); Foreign Languages Press for extracts from *Fundamental Issues in Present-Day China* by Deng Xiaoping (1987).

The Publishers would like to thank the following to reproduce copyright illustrations in this volume:

Page 22 Xinhua News Agency (New China Pictures Company); Page 68 Xinhua News Agency (New China Pictures Company); Page 79 Popperfoto/Reuters; Page 81 Popperfoto/Reuters; Page 115 Xinhua News Agency (New China Pictures Company).

Every effort has been made to trace and acknowledge ownership of copyright. The Publishers will be glad to make suitable arrangements with copyright holders whom it has not been possible to contact.

1 Introduction: Communist China

On 1 October 1949 Mao Zedong (Mao Tse-tung), Chairman of the Chinese Communist Party, stood on a balcony of the old imperial palace in Beijing (Peking) to proclaim the formal establishment of the People's Republic of China (PRC). His pronouncement marked the final victory of the Chinese Communists over their enemies after two decades of civil war. The internal development of the People's Republic during the ensuing half-century and the impact this had on world affairs provide the themes of this book. However, in order to put the story of Communist China in context it is first necessary to introduce the main features of Chinese history and to outline the events that led to the triumph of Mao Zedong and his followers.

1 Background

By tradition China was a profoundly conservative nation. Its principal shaping influence had been Confucianism, a philosophy which emphasised the need for harmony in human relations and enjoined the Chinese people to accept without complaint their place in an unchanging social order. Such quietism had produced a hierarchical structure in which the first duty of the citizen was to obey lawful authority, expressed in its highest political form in the rule of the emperor whose right to govern derived from his being the recipient of 'the mandate of heaven'. This notion, which was broadly equivalent to the European concept of the divine right of kings, gave legitimacy to the holders of power and justified their suppression of all opposition.

China's conservatism was also reflected in its attitude towards the outside world. Until the nineteenth century China had essentially been a closed society. For over two thousand years it had deliberately avoided contact with other nations wherever possible. Largely isolated from foreign influences, it had developed a deep sense of its own superiority over all other cultures. However, this self-belief was suddenly and profoundly shaken in the 1840s when a number of Western industrial nations, principally Britain and France, used their greater military strength and more advanced technology to impose themselves on China. The Chinese were forced to open their ports to foreign commerce and to enter into a series of 'unequal treaties' which obliged them to surrender sovereign territory and accept trade on Western terms. By 1900 over fifty Chinese 'treaty ports' were in foreign possession. Chinese bitterness at such humiliation created mounting dissatisfaction with the imperial government. The Qing (Manchu) dynasty's inability to protect China encouraged the growth of a revolutionary movement. The remarkable feature of this movement was its desire to achieve 'a revolution against the world to join the world', to end China's subjection to the West by adopting progressive Western political and economic ways.

In 1911 China underwent the first of its modern revolutions when the Qing government collapsed. Although a republic was set up in place of the imperial system, it was unclear where the real power in China now lay. For the next forty years rival war lords and factions struggled to assert authority. Two main revolutionary parties were in contention: the Nationalists or Guomindang (GMD) created by Sun Yatsen and led after 1925 by Chiang Kaishek (Jiang Jieshi), and the Chinese Communist Party (CCP), whose leader from the later 1920s was Mao Zedong. Although the Guomindang (Kuomintang) was the nominal government of China from the early 1930s, it was never able to crush its Communist rivals. Moreover, such power as the Nationalists had was seriously compromised after 1931 by their irresolute response to the military occupation of many of the richest and most densely populated parts of the Chinese mainland by China's neighbour and traditional enemy, Japan. In contrast to Chiang Kaishek's lack of fight, Mao Zedong led the CCP from its bases in Jiangxi (Kiansi) and Yanan (Yenan) in a spirited resistance to the Japanese occupation. Mao's main strategy was to win over the peasants who made up 80 per cent of the Chinese population. His success in this had the double effect of providing military recruits for the anti-Japanese struggle and political supporters for the CCP in its campaign against the urban-based Nationalists.

With the defeat of Japan at the end of the Second World War in 1945, the CCP turned on the GMD in a renewal of the civil war that had lasted intermittently since the late 1920s. A fierce four-year struggle for supremacy ended with the complete victory of the Communists. By 1949 the Guomindang had been driven from the Chinese mainland; their one remaining stronghold was the offshore island of Taiwan (Formosa). Mao and the CCP were now in a position to establish Communist rule over the whole of mainland China.

(For a fuller analysis of the pre-1949 developments readers should consult the companion volume to this book, *From Empire to People's Republic: China 1900-49.*)

2 The Shape of Chinese History Since 1949

a) The Consolidation of Communist Authority, 1949-57

During the Jiangxi and Yanan periods of the 1930s and 1940s, Mao Zedong, by a combination of political and military skill, luck, and utter ruthlessness, had succeeded in imposing his personal authority on the CCP. His dominance became even greater with the creation of the People's Republic of China in 1949. Between then and his death in 1976, Mao Zedong was revered by the mass of the Chinese people as a living god. But the adulation which was lavished on him could not

The provinces of China with their main towns and cities

hide the huge problems he faced as leader of the new China. His most demanding task was to bring stability to a nation that had been riven by decades of division and turmoil. Mao's political approach was a simple one; he would tolerate no opposition to the CCP. All other parties were outlawed and the total obedience of the nation to the new government was demanded.

Initially, the officials and public figures who had previously served the GMD Nationalist government but had not fled to Taiwan were asked by the Communist authorities to stay in their posts. They were promised that if they committed themselves to the new China they would suffer no retaliation for their past behaviour. For a short period this undertaking was honoured, but once the officials had served their purpose by providing the young PRC with the necessary continuity of administration they were turned on and persecuted as class enemies.

The concept of class enemies was basic to the social and political strategies of the Communists in government. Invoking the traditional Chinese duty to respect authority, Mao and the CCP leaders began public campaigns of vilification against anyone in public life who opposed official policy. From 1950 onwards an atmosphere of fear and uncertainty was systematically created by a series of 'anti-movements', launched against those whom the CCP regarded as socially or politically suspect. The Chinese people were urged to expose all who had co-operated with the former GMD government. China became a nation of informers. It was enough for individuals to be charged by their neighbours with having belonged to the privileged classes for them to be publicly denounced and to have their property seized. Their avowals of loyalty to the new socialist China were ignored. The vengeful atmosphere was intensified by China's being drawn into the Korean War (1950-53). This struggle placed great demands on the new regime and provided further pretexts for the government to harry the population. Some of the worst excesses occurred in the countryside where millions of landlords were brutally dispossessed of their lands which were then redistributed among the peasants.

Purges were also carried out within the CCP. Members suspected of not totally following the party line were condemned as 'rightists' who were opposed to the progress of the PRC. Purges were alternated with periods when party members were encouraged to criticise current policies. This apparent liberalising was invariably followed by the imposition of even tougher restrictions on freedom of expression. A striking example occurred in 1957 when Mao, using the slogan 'Let a hundred flowers bloom; let a hundred schools of thought contend', called on members to air their grievances. Those who were rash enough to do so were then attacked as 'rightists'. Such purges were to become a recurrent feature of Chinese politics down to Mao's death in 1976.

b) The Great Leap Forward, 1958-66

In economic matters Mao's basic aim was to industrialise China. He hoped that within a short period the new China would be able to match the Soviet Union and the capitalist West in industrial output. To achieve this he copied the Stalinist model of a series of five-year plans. These involved prodigious physical efforts by the Chinese workers, but, since Mao deliberately chose to place his faith in mass labour rather than in advanced technology, the plans were only partially successful. The limitations of Mao's approach were particularly evident during the Second Five-Year Plan (1958-62). Intended to be 'the Great Leap Forward', the Plan fell far short of its production targets. The true figures of the failure were hidden from the people, but what the authorities could not conceal was the widespread famine that accompanied the Plan. The collapse of the food supply system was directly attributable to two factors, collectivisation and 'Lysenkoism'. The land which had been given to the peasants after its seizure from the landlords had to be forfeited in a mass collectivisation programme which ended private ownership. The dislocation this caused was made worse by Mao's decision to implement in China the specious crop-production theories of the Soviet agronomist, Trofim Lysenko (see page 29). This combination of social disruption and flawed science produced a catastrophe throughout China. Deaths were numbered in millions.

Characteristically, Mao declined to acknowledge responsibility for the famine, but in the early 1960s he withdrew into the political background, leaving two prominent party figures, Deng Xiaoping (Teng Hsiao-ping) and Liu Shaoqi (Liu Shao-chi), to tackle the problem of food shortages. Their attempts to repair the economic damage led them to reverse some of Mao's earlier policies. One key adjustment was the abandonment of collectivisation. Mao was considerably disturbed by this since he saw it as an undermining of the socialist principles on which China's 1949 revolution rested. In a series of dramatic gestures, which included his swimming in the Yangzi (Yangste) river, the ageing Chairman reappeared in public and reasserted his dominance in Chinese politics. What inspired him to return was the fear that had always moved him, and which increased as he grew older, that the revolution he had led might not survive his death. He determined, therefore, to impose a political and social structure on China that would permanently define its character as a nation. This was the intention behind his introduction in 1966 of the great Cultural Revolution, an extraordinary movement that plunged China into a decade of deliberately engineered turmoil.

c) The Cultural Revolution 1966-76

Mao's objective in unleashing the Cultural Revolution was to oblige the Party to acknowledge all its current errors and in so doing purge itself of all possible rivals to his authority. His chosen instrument for achieving this was the youth of China. In 1966 he called upon the young to set themselves up in judgement over their elders. He urged them to form a mass movement to destroy the 'four olds' that were threatening China's revolution - 'old culture, old thoughts, old customs and old habits'. The young people responded with an idealistic enthusiasm that soon degenerated into a brutal fanaticism. Squads of teenagers, known as Red Guards, rampaged through China's cities and towns, seizing and assaulting those whom they regarded as the 'bad elements' representing China's corrupt past. No part of China's antique culture was sacred. Buildings - whether universities, libraries, museums or temples - which in the eyes of the Red Guards stood as memorials to Chinese decadence were smashed or burned.

The violence was part of a wholesale attack upon China's traditional culture. All forms of artistic expression were subjected to crippling censorship. They had to pass the test of 'socialist integrity' imposed by Mao's wife, Jiang Qing (Chiang Ching), who was entrusted with the responsibility for recreating Chinese culture. In the event she achieved the reverse. Her demand that all forms of creativity must conform absolutely with her notions of true socialist culture meant that nothing of lasting significance was produced or presented. China became an artistic wilderness.

The Cultural Revolution was an act of madness but there was method in it. The Red Guards were a highly visible and terrifying feature of the movement but they were essentially a front. Mao was using the apparent anarchy to enforce his will upon the CCP and the nation. It was a means of fulfilling his concept of 'continuing revolution', the belief that unless the Communist Party was regularly purified it would cease to be a revolutionary force and China would cease to be truly socialist. For ten years after 1966 the Cultural Revolution severely distorted China both internally and in its relations with the outside world.

In foreign affairs a particularly significant development was the PRC's deepening estrangement from the USSR. In its early years the PRC had looked upon the Soviet Union as its mentor and had sided with it as a natural ally in the East-West Cold War. But China's growing realisation that it was being financially and commercially exploited by the Soviet Union, which refused to accept China as an equal partner in the international revolutionary movement, led to profound mutual hostility in the 1960s. The Cultural Revolution served to confirm Soviet fears that the PRC under Mao had abandoned realism and rationality.

By 1976, after a decade of Cultural Revolution, there were signs that even Mao himself considered the social and political extremism had gone too far. What he actually thought of the Cultural Revolution and its consequences cannot be easily assessed since for the last part of his life his physical decline meant he could barely articulate his ideas. As he grew frailer a power struggle developed behind the scenes. With his death in September 1976 this became an open conflict. There were three principal contestants: the Gang of Four, a small group of hard-liners led by Mao's widow, Jiang Qing; the moderate Hua Guofeng (Hua Kuo-feng) whom Mao had nominated as his successor; and the wily pragmatist, Deng Xiaoping, who had survived being purged and demoted during the Cultural Revolution. The Gang of Four lacked a power base and were unpopular with the military. Within weeks of Mao's death they had been outmanoeuvred and imprisoned. For two years Hua was the nominal leader of China but since he never acquired the total support of the CCP there was little chance of his inheriting Mao's full authority. By 1979 Hua had been superseded by Deng, who now emerged as the major force in Chinese politics.

d) The Deng Revolution, 1976-89

Once he had gained the leadership, Deng Xiaoping initiated a remarkable change of direction in China's economic and foreign policies. Even in Mao's time there had been signs that China was unhappy with its international isolation. Its bitter rivalry with the USSR over the leadership of the Communist world had led the PRC to cultivate better relations with the West. In the years before his death in 1976, Zhou Enlai (Chou En-lai), the PRC's foreign secretary and veteran statesman, had played a prominent role in improving China's diplomatic contacts. It was Zhou who helped prise open the 'bamboo curtain', the Asian equivalent of the 'iron curtain' in Europe. The visit of the American president, Richard Nixon, to China in 1972 was a celebrated example of the success of Zhou's diplomacy. Deng Xiaoping hoped to build on Zhou's achievements. His declared intention was to 'open China to the world'.

Improved foreign relations were part of a broad strategy that became known as 'the Deng Revolution'. This was essentially a set of policies aimed at modernising China's economy. The striking feature was that while the nation was to remain nominally socialist it would embrace capitalist methods whenever these were judged likely to bring practical benefits. In a landmark decision of the Eleventh Party Congress in 1978, the CCP resolved that the economy would in future be structured along utilitarian not ideological lines. Deng announced a programme of 'four modernisations' (in agriculture, industry, defence and education) which were intended to push China towards eventual parity with the West. On the agricultural front, collectivisation was abandoned, individual ownership of land was permitted, and peasants were allowed to sell their produce privately as well as to the state. Industry was stimulated by the adoption of Western production techniques. Workers were given incentives by the introduction of differential earnings to replace the previous fixed state wages. Special Economic Zones (SEZ), modelled on successful Western practice, were created with the specific task of increasing China's international trade.

An extraordinary feature of Deng Xiaoping's revolution was that he had no intention of accompanying the sweeping economic reforms with comparable political changes. Indeed, Deng purposefully set his face against such a notion. He reasserted the absolute right of the Chinese Communist Party to govern China unchallenged. It was this intransigence that deepened political disaffection and led to the development during the 1980s of a pro-democracy movement in China.

The movement was strongest among the nation's intellectuals, who were just beginning to recover from the assault on them in the Cultural Revolution. It campaigned for a fifth modernisation - democracy - to be added to Deng's other four. Confrontations between the authorities and the democrats were frequent throughout the 1980s. The climax came in 1989 in Beijing when a pro-democracy demonstration in Tiananmen Square was violently dispersed by government forces.

e) China Since 1989

Although the Chinese government's action in Tiananmen Square aroused worldwide condemnation, there was no concerted international effort to apply sanctions in response. China's commercial relations with the outside world were not seriously harmed. In fact, international events at this juncture combined to ease China's way forward. The collapse of Communism in the Soviet bloc in Europe, which began in the late 1980s, effectively ended the Cold War. This had the immediate consequence for the PRC of lessening the tensions that had existed between it and the Western nations. Of equal significance was the disintegration of the USSR in 1991. There was now no longer a Sino-Soviet struggle for the leadership of world Communism. China's belief that these remarkable international developments offered it new opportunities appeared justified by the figures which showed a notable increase in the 1990s in the PRC's trade with the USA and Europe. Furthermore, the handover by Britain of Hong Kong in 1997 on terms which were very close to the PRC's original demands occasioned great rejoicing in China. As well as bringing a major economic and financial resource under China's control, the recovery of Hong Kong had profound symbolism for the Chinese people. They viewed it as effectively marking the end of one hundred and fifty years of Western imperialism in China.

With the return of Macao (Macau) from the Portuguese scheduled for 1999, the PRC's only remaining territorial demand was for

Taiwan. But this was a much more difficult problem to solve. Britain and Portugal had never sought to deny the ultimate right of China to reclaim Hong Kong and Macao. In contrast, the offshore island of Taiwan, which had been held by the GMD since 1949, rejected the PRC's demand for its reincorporation into mainland China. It is true that relations between the PRC and the Taiwan government had improved since the 1970s and that considerable, if unofficial, trade had developed between the two countries. But on the question of sovereignty neither side would budge; both claimed an exclusive right over Taiwan. As the twentieth century drew to a close all the signs were that the Taiwan issue would continue to cause severe friction. Short of a military settlement being imposed by one side on the other, there appeared to be no realistic prospect of the question being resolved.

Despite its broad measure of success in foreign affairs, China faced mounting domestic problems. Between his ordering of the Tiananmen repression in 1989 and his death in 1997, Deng struggled to keep a balance between the rightists in the CCP who wanted to push China towards total Westernisation and the leftists who would not accept capitalism at any price. It was a problem that he passed on unsettled to his successors.

3 China and the Historians

China has always had chroniclers of its history, but it has no tradition of historical writing as the term is understood in the West. The ascertaining of facts and the pursuit of objectivity and balance are largely alien to the Chinese. The ruling authorities have always required that writers and commentators when describing the past do so in such a way that reflects well on the present. Indeed, to the Chinese the purpose of history is to justify the present. What facilitates this is that written Chinese has no past tense; historical events are necessarily expressed in the present tense. This imparts to historical accounts a sense of immediacy which can make them appear strikingly relevant. It is a legacy of an antique culture that went unchanged for so long that it thought of itself in terms of a continuous present rather than of a linear development.

After the creation of the People's Republic of China in 1949, the Communist authorities continued the practice of controlling all official publications. The news media in the PRC have always been heavily centralised. The state controls 85 per cent of the output of the Chinese press. This means that the media are effectively the mouthpiece of the Beijing government, whose policies are invariably greeted with universal approval from China's newspapers and journals. The line established by Xinhua (Hsinhua), the PRC's official news agency, is toed both by the mass circulation dailies and by the internationally published Chinese newspapers and journals.

During the half-century of the PRC's existence after 1949 nothing was printed in these papers or in any other official publication that was critical of the CCP's record or its policies in government. Before 1976, all that appeared was in effect hagiography, lauding Mao Zedong and the CCP and condemning China's internal and foreign enemies. With the death of Mao in 1976 and the subsequent decline in his reputation, a number of adjustments to the official record were made. But these were very limited. There was no equivalent to the de-Stalinisation that occurred in the USSR in the wake of Stalin's death in 1953. The ensuing power-struggle between the conservative Maoists, such as the 'Gang of Four', and the more progressive Communists who believed that changes were necessary for Party and national survival, resulted in the defeat of the die-hards. But this did not leave the victors entirely free to reject Maoism. If the members of the CCP had admitted that serious mistakes had been made by the Party under Mao's direction it would have undermined their own standing.

So the CCP adopted a form of compromise. In 1981 at a special congress the CCP passed a formal resolution declaring that Mao had been the true founder of Communist China but had been '70 per cent right and 30 per cent wrong' in his subsequent policies. This strange quantification was meant to provide a flexible formula which would enable the PRC to abandon without further explanation those Maoist ideas which they now found embarrassing or irrelevant. Mao could not be rejected entirely by his successors; after all, they had risen to prominence under him and had carried out the Cultural Revolution on his orders. But Deng Xiaoping in introducing his own revolution was eager that China should deliberately overlook those aspects of its recent past which it could not undo. He let it be known that the Cultural Revolution was now to be regarded as a closed book.

The Chinese responded by showing their traditional capacity for ignoring inconvenient facts. The result has been that the Cultural Revolution, the great centre piece of Chinese history since 1949, is now largely ignored in China. Politicians deliberately avoid referring to it and students are seldom taught about it. The present writer's own experience of trying to engage the Chinese on this subject is of being met with an inscrutable smile and a polite but firm indication that they would much prefer to talk about something else. Middle-aged men and women who were once Red Guards will sometimes own up to the fact, but they will wearily explain that it is a topic that no longer interests them.

It is important to stress that the disruption caused by the Cultural Revolution was more than an interlude in the development of modern China. The Maoists had made a deliberate attempt to destroy China's past. Rigid censorship had rendered analytical writing impossible in any meaningful sense during that period. This, together with the closing of the universities and the physical destruction of archives and libraries, had a disastrous effect on scholarship. Historians had neither the freedom nor the means to pursue their craft. Even after Mao had died and the orgy of cultural devastation had ended, his successors made no serious attempt to repair the damage. Indeed, strict censorship continued to operate. In 1996 Dr Jao Yu, one of a small band of unofficial historians still trying to follow their profession, attempted to publish an analysis of the Cultural Revolution to coincide with the thirtieth anniversary of its beginning. He found that he could not get his work past the censors who continued to operate as effectively, albeit less brutally, under Deng as they had under Mao. Jao reflected sadly: 'The Cultural Revolution happened thirty years ago and ended twenty years ago. Now we should do a lot of things to study the Cultural Revolution, to study the purpose, the outcome, but there is nothing. No conference, no meeting, no symposium. So nothing'.

Another writer Jiang Wun, (Chiang Wun) bemoaned the readiness of the Chinese people to remain intellectually oppressed:

1 I just feel the Chinese people are inclined to forget things too easily. They are also ready to accept whatever they are told as gospel. There is never any discussion. There are only conclusions. If we have such a simplistic response to this ten-year movement then it is possible for
5 such a revolution to take place again. If we adopt over simplistic solutions to one mistake, we may make even bigger mistakes in future.

Frances Wood, a long-time resident in Beijing and curator of the Chinese collection at the British Museum in London, emphasised the stunted quality of current Chinese interest in history:

1 If one talks about respect for the past or interest in the past, I think that's very low in China. Interest in the traditional culture is restricted to a tiny minority. There is just no sensitivity to the past and I think that has a lot to do with the Cultural Revolution. In the Cultural Revolution
5 the past was uniformly regarded as a bad thing. There was nothing to be got from it and, whilst you might have hoped perhaps for a sort of reversion to a kind of sentimentality about the past, that is one of the things that hasn't come back. I think it is partly to do with the fact that the people were so badly educated. It's an enormous loss to China in many
10 ways.

Others have noted that the attack upon truth and openness did not end with Mao Zedong's passing. Reflecting on a violent crackdown in 1983 by the PRC on the pro-democracy movement, Yang Lien, one of China's major poets, pointed out that suppression and control of information were basic to the tradition of Chinese government:

1 After 1976 people hoped that the Cultural Revolution was over. With chairman Mao dead and Hua Guofeng and Deng Xiaoping in power, people took the view that the Cultural Revolution had been a peculiar kind of nightmare, but with the campaign [in 1983] against spiritual

5 pollution the newspapers and television broadcasts suddenly filled up
with all that familiar and terrifying language and ideology, just like in the
Cultural Revolution, and the intellectual community was thrown back
into the despair of the worst days. But, whereas before they had been
10 following blindly, this time they were open eyed. So, suddenly they
realised that the Cultural Revolution wasn't a short-term, one-off
phenomenon, it had deeper roots, roots which must be faced up to.

Those Chinese who had been prepared to give their loyalty to the
post-Mao leadership in the hope that it would direct China along less
oppressive paths were deeply disillusioned by the regime's crushing of
the pro-democracy demonstration in Beijing in June 1989. Jung Lei, a
journalist, concluded that the new Communist government under
Deng was as repressive as the previous one under Mao had been. Jung
had earlier unearthed evidence of widespread cannibalism during the
Cultural Revolution, but had been reluctant to publish the story for
fear of embarrassing Deng's government. The Tiananmen Square
massacre removed his qualms:

1 At the time I thought these things were very shocking, but since the
Communist Party was trying to introduce reforms I didn't want to
embarrass them. I thought writing a factual piece would be too stark
and cruel, so I intended to write a piece of fiction. But then came the
5 massacre of 1989 and I came to a deeper understanding of the essence
of Communist rule. I completely despaired of it and I decided to write
a factual account to make people fully aware of the cruel events which
had taken place under the Communists.

Roderick MacFarquhar, the leading Western analyst of the Cultural
Revolution, offered the following explanation of China's reluctance
to face its recent past:

1 When Deng Xiaoping decided to open China to the West, I think he
recognised it was an exhausted nation. It was completely exhausted by
political campaigns and living on nothing but promises - not even
promises, but just living on exhortation and heroism which didn't really
5 benefit any individual. I think he realised there was this desire for a
better life and I think that was the sort of great engine for what's
happened in China since. What they didn't do in that resolution [of
1981 declaring Mao 70 per cent right, 30 per cent wrong] and what I
think that we in the West can still help in doing is to take apart the
10 details and to analyse more deeply the way in which Mao plotted the
whole Cultural Revolution, because I think that's what isn't clear from
the Chinese account, the way in which step by step he took apart the
top ranks of the Party before launching the Cultural Revolution and we
are only now beginning to put it together, because the Chinese them-
15 selves while they issue material which is relevant to that appraisal do
not make that appraisal themselves.

Scholars in China struggling to re-establish the means of academic inquiry admit that they face an enormous task. They also acknowledged the truth of MacFarquhar's observation that the Chinese in order to rediscover their own history have to look to the West for vital information and insights. For example, the death tolls relating to the great famine of the 1950s and to the Cultural Revolution are drawn from Western computations.

It is evident from all this that Chinese academics who are desperate for information about their own history tend to rely on foreign sinologists for enlightenment. This obviously throws a great responsibility on non-Chinese historians, particularly those in the West, since it is mainly to Western authorities that the Chinese turn. Here a particular difficulty applies. Keen though Western historians have been to convey the truth about China, they have necessarily tended to interpret Chinese history very much from the standpoint of the West. The history of the PRC coincided with the Cold War. For much of that time China was looked upon as the ally of the USSR and therefore as an intractable enemy of Western interests. The American attitude in this respect is particularly instructive. The Communist victory in China in 1949 forced the USA, which had invested so much diplomacy and capital in east Asia before 1949, to reappraise Chinese history. A large number of universities in the USA established departments of Chinese studies in the 1950s. Their concern was to explain what they regarded as a Cold War calamity, the 'loss' of China to Mao's Communists and the forming of a Communist bloc between the PRC and the Soviet Union.

Yet, whatever the political motives behind it, the American initiative produced some outstanding scholarship which made a major contribution to Western understanding of China. Particularly distinguished American sinologists were Stuart Schram, the first major Western biographer of Mao Zedong, Orville Schell, who produced invaluable collections and translations of Chinese documents, and John King Fairbank whose published studies of China placed the PRC in the wider context of Chinese historical development. British historians also contributed significantly to the study of China. Prominent among them were Roderick MacFarqhuar, acknowledged as the greatest English-speaking authority on the Cultural Revolution, and the prolific Jonathan Spence whose analyses of China's transition from an antique culture to a modern state have become required reading worldwide.

The outstanding attribute of these historians was their objectivity. Their endeavour was always to treat the Chinese record in as balanced a form as possible. Both the positive and negative aspects of the PRC were presented. Their approach was a valuable corrective to the one-sided accounts that had been produced earlier by writers who were committed to a particular ideological viewpoint. For example, at the height of the Cold War many American-based studies had been compromised by their too evident distaste for Communism, whether in its Russian or Chinese form. There had been equal distortions at the opposite end of the political spectrum. Left-wing radicals, most notably in France and the USA, had lionised Mao Zedong as a great liberator whose progressive brand of Communism had superseded the atrophied Soviet variety. It took a generation before such Western liberals were prepared to accept the truth about the horrors of the Great Leap Forward and the Cultural Revolution.

Cold War divisions created a particular difficulty for Western historians attempting to write accurate accounts of Chinese history. The former USSR is a major repository of sources on China, and Soviet collections of documents are thus essential to a full analysis of the history of the PRC. However, in the Cold War atmosphere the Soviet experts on China were either unwilling or were not permitted to co-operate with their Western counterparts. It was not until after the break-up of the USSR in the early 1990s that Western scholars were granted access to Soviet archives. By the late 1990s co-operation between Western and Russian historians had begun to throw light on many previously hidden aspects of both the domestic and international history of the PRC. The ways in which these scholarly contacts have altered Western perceptions of such matters as China's involvement in the Korean War, the Sino-Soviet struggle for the leadership of international communism, and the Chinese attempt to head the anti-colonial struggle are detailed in later chapters of this book.

4 Issues in Chinese History Since 1949

A number of critical questions dominate the history of China after 1949. They divide themselves into four main categories: economics, politics, ideology and foreign affairs.

a) Economics

In 1949 the biggest task facing the PRC was simply one of survival. It was by no means certain that the CCP government would be able to surmount the economic difficulties that had weakened China for over a century and had helped to bring down the previous Nationalist government. China was a predominantly rural society, 80 per cent of its people being peasants. It did not have the base for building a modern industrial nation. Some commentators argue that so great were China's economic problems that had the PRC not been led by a government with absolute authority and totally dedicated to survival, the nation would have been overwhelmed. According to this line of argument, the absolutism which the CCP under Mao exercised over China was essential. The institutions and infrastructure simply did not exist to enable China to evolve towards modernity. If there was to be survival, let alone progress, the means had to be imposed and directed from above. The collectivisation and industrialisation programmes that Mao enforced may not have accorded with civil rights as understood and operated in other nations but China's needs made them unavoidable. According to this interpretation, Mao's harsh and dictatorial ways between 1949 and 1976 saved China from disintegration and laid the basis for the 'revolution' of the 1980s, when Deng Xiaoping was able to build the four modernisations upon the hard-won achievements of the Maoist years. Others have taken issue with this form of reasoning and have asserted that, rather than laying a foundation for growth, Mao's economic policies condemned China to continued backwardness; it was not until Deng abandoned those policies that China was able to take the first steps towards becoming a modern industrial nation.

b) Politics

The major question facing the PRC at the time of its creation was how could it establish the stability and permanence that had eluded all the regimes since the fall of the Qings in 1911. The short answer was by a successful return to absolutism. The political character of China after 1949 has occasioned much debate. It is possible to argue that the PRC was no different in essentials from traditional Chinese political systems. Despite its title, the People's Republic, the PRC allowed no involvement in government by the vast majority of the people. The rule of the CCP was as uncompromising and self-perpetuating as that of the emperors. Maoist China was not, therefore, a new China except in certain outward appearances. The change in 1949 was one of form rather than of substance. Despite its revolutionary claims, China remained a politically reactionary society. All authority came from the top and the people's duty was to obey. However, a counter viewpoint exists: it is that Maoism did indeed alter the fundamentals of Chinese government. Mao introduced into China something it had not known before - the concept of continuing revolution. He may have retained the traditional methods of Chinese political authoritarianism but his purpose was to change the character of China by making it conform to his particular notion of Marxist revolution. It can be further argued that the permanence of what Mao had done was evident in Deng Xiaoping's decision to leave the essentials of Mao's political system unaltered. At every point in Deng's revolution he insisted on the right and necessity of the CCP's continuing to govern China unchallenged. The government's suppression of the democracy movement in Tiananmen Square in 1989 and its subsequent severities were very much in keeping with the Maoist hardline tradition.

c) Ideology

The debate on the political character of China after 1949 raises the question of the PRC's relationship to the international Communist movement. Some observers accept that Red China genuinely attempted to replace the Soviet Union at the head of international Communism in order to lead the world into revolution. Others reject this and argue that China's aims were national not international. They claim, as Moscow did at the height of the Sino-Soviet conflict in the 1960s, that Chinese Communism, far from being a truly international Marxist force, was merely a brand of national self-assertion. This was illustrated by the peremptory way in which the PRC went about its self-proclaimed task of leading the forces of anti-colonialism. Rather than deal with the emergent nations as equal partners, China required them to subordinate themselves to Chinese interests. This lends weight to the notion that Marxism had been embraced by Chinese revolutionaries not because of its appeal to proletarian brotherhood but because it offered a means of restoring China's sense of self-worth and greatness after a century of foreign domination. The attraction of Marxism to the Chinese was not philosophical but practical; it provided a programme for China's regeneration as a nation. It is sometimes suggested that the Chinese belief in 'Marxism-Leninism-Maoism' did not long survive the death of Mao, but that Deng and his successors in government retained it as a formal ideology for the very good reason that it was the only justification for their continuance in power.

d) Foreign Affairs

Initially, Western observers tended to interpret the PRC as a major Communist power, which, in league with the USSR, was aggressively pursuing international Marxist revolution. However, what is now often emphasised is that throughout the period of Mao's leadership of the PRC it was fear that shaped his attitude towards the outside world. Mao's abiding anxiety was that the West, led by the United States, was preparing to attack China. This led him to divert the greater part of China's resources to creating an internal defence system and to developing Chinese atomic weapons. In the eyes of a number of commentators Mao's fears verged on the paranoid and prevented the PRC from following a rational or balanced foreign policy. This was particularly evident at the time of the Cultural Revolution when Maoist fanaticism made it virtually impossible for other nations to conduct diplomatic relations with China. Yet without denying the restrictions that Mao's anxieties placed on China's foreign policy it is possible to suggest that his achievement remains considerable. Mao, after all, made the PRC a superpower. At his death China possessed a weight and influence in international affairs that was unprecedented in its history. Much of that had been due to the statesmanship of Zhou Enlai, who as China's foreign minister had helped to re-establish better relations with the USA and the Western world. After 1976 Deng Xiaoping built upon the foundations laid by Zhou. By the 1990s Deng's policy of opening China to the world had put the PRC on better terms internationally than at any time since its foundation in 1949.

The key issues in economics, politics, ideology and foreign affairs provide the material and main themes of the following chapters. Of course, it should be stressed that, while it is convenient to deal with them as separate factors, the overlap and interaction between them is constant and considerable.

Working on the 'Introduction'

Your aim in reading this chapter should be to gain a basic grasp of the following:
1. the principal features of Chinese politics and society before 1949;
2. the main developments in the history of the PRC since 1949, arranged in chronological order;
3. the problems confronting Chinese and Western scholars in studying the history of the PRC;
4. the key issues in the history of the PRC.

Try writing brief answers to the following questions. This will reveal whether or not you have grasped the essential points.
1. Why had the Chinese Communists emerged victorious over the Nationalists by 1949?
2. What were the main features of a) the CCP's consolidation of its authority in China between 1949 and 1966, b) the Cultural Revolution, 1966-76, c) the Deng Revolution, 1976-89, and d) developments in China between 1989 and 1997?
3. In what ways did the Cold War distort Western understanding of the history of the PRC?
4. Under the headings 'economics', 'politics', 'ideology' and 'foreign affairs' identify the key issues in the history of the PRC.

2 China Under Mao: Politics and Economics, 1949-66

1 The Consolidation of Communist Power, 1949-53

The creation of the People's Republic of China marked the successful climax of a twenty-year struggle. Against immense odds Mao had led China into a new era. For the first time in a century China was free of foreign domination, the Nationalists had been driven off the Chinese mainland and Mao, as head of the CCP, was now in a position to impose his concept of socialism on the new republic.

He moved cautiously at first, seeking broad acceptance for his policies. It is true that the property of those nationalists who had fled with Chiang Kaishek to Taiwan was seized and the banks and public utilities - gas, electricity and transport - were brought under state control. All foreign assets, save those of the USSR, were also taken over. But the new regime was prepared to offer compensation to those former owners and share holders who declared their willingness to work in the new China. Mao announced that the PRC was ready to use the resources of these 'national capitalists' to fund China's development as a 'socialist-agrarian-industrial' society.

He was also aware that, although the Chinese middle classes were a numerically small part of an overwhelmingly peasant population, their significance outweighed their numbers. It was they who provided the officials, the civil servants and the industrial managers. Those who had been unwilling or unable to flee with the defeated Guomindang were invited to stay in their positions and become loyal servants of the new government. Many judged it opportune to do so and these were augmented by a number of expatriate Chinese who returned from abroad in a spirit of idealism, eager to serve the new regime.

For administrative purposes, the country was divided into six regions, each governed by a bureau of four major officials; chairman, party secretary, military commander and political commissar (see the map on page 19). Since the last two posts were filled by officers of the People's Liberation Army (PLA), this effectively left China under military control, a situation which Mao Zedong considered offered the best means of stabilising China and guaranteeing the continued rule of the Chinese Communist Party. The overarching governmental power resided in the Central People's Government Council. This was composed of fifty-six leading party members, the majority of whom were veterans of the Yanan years. Six of these served as vice-chairmen under Mao who, as Chairman of the Council, was the dominant figure.

A problem requiring the new government's immediate attention

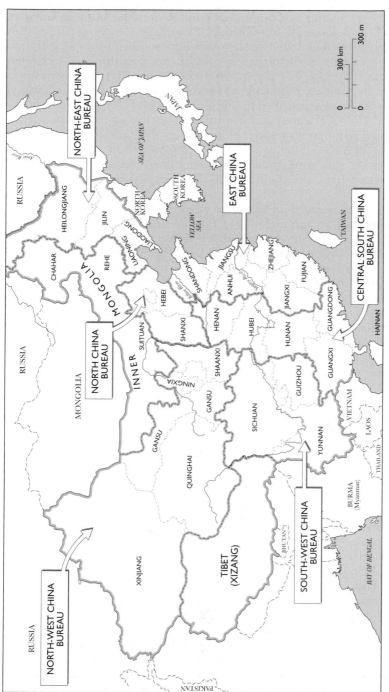

The administrative divisions of the PRC

was the enforcing of Communist control over the outlying areas of China. In a series of 'reunification' campaigns three separate PLA armies were despatched west, north and south. One was sent into Tibet (Xizang) in October 1950; within six months it had crushed Tibetan resistance (see pages 106–108). Similar PLA ruthlessness was shown in Xinjiang (Sinkiang). This distant northern province, which bordered Soviet-controlled Outer Mongolia, had a large Muslim population. The CCP feared that it would either declare its independence of China or fall prey to Soviet incursion. By 1951, within a year of their arrival, PLA detachments had imposed Communist control over the region. At the same time, the Guangdong (Kwantung) region in southern China, the traditional GMD base, was brought under PLA control.

This swift assertion of its military power enabled the CCP to direct its attention to administrative reform and social reconstruction. Conscious of the nepotism and self-seeking that had severely weakened the efficiency and morale of the Nationalist government, Mao made a particular point of attacking corruption. In 1951, in keeping with the Chinese love for classifying programmes under cardinal numbers, he declared the beginning of 'the Three Anti-Movement', the targets being waste, corruption and inefficiency. This was expanded in 1952 into 'the Five Anti-Movement', which was intended to stimulate the economy by attacking industrial sabotage, tax evasion, bribery, fraud, and theft of government property. Its main aim was to destroy the remnants of what Mao defined as 'the bureaucratic capitalist class'. It was clear that three years after the Communist takeover Mao felt able to turn against the classes which he had earlier tolerated in order to keep China's civil service functioning. In 1952, in a widely broadcast public statement, 'On People's Democratic Dictatorship', Mao justified his tough line:

1 Our present task is to strengthen the people's state apparatus - meaning principally the people's army, the people's police and the people's courts - thereby safeguarding national defence and protecting the people's interests. Given these conditions, China, under the leadership of the
5 working class and the Communist Party, can develop steadily from an agricultural into an industrial country and from a New Democratic into a Socialist and, eventually, Communist society, eliminating classes and realizing universal harmony.

Such state apparatus as the army, the police and the courts are
10 instruments with which one class oppresses another. As far as the hostile classes are concerned, these are instruments of oppression. They are violent and certainly not 'benevolent' things.

We definitely have no benevolent policies towards the reactionaries or the counter-revolutionary activities of the reactionary classes. Our
15 benevolent policy does not apply to such deeds or such persons, who are outside the ranks of the people; it applies only to the people.

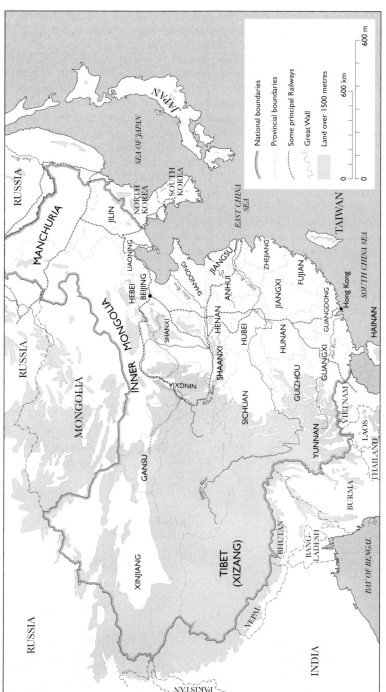

The outlying provinces of China

> The people's state is for the protection of the people. Once they
> have a people's state, the people then have the possibility of applying
> democratic methods on a nationwide and comprehensive scale to
> 20 educate and reform themselves, so that they may get rid of the influ-
> ences of domestic and foreign reactionaries.

These policies were to be applied in urban China. In the countryside,
Mao reintroduced the policy that had characterised the rule of the
Communists in the 'liberated' areas in the Jiangxi and Yanan periods.
Reforms were implemented in 1950 which forced the landlords to
give up their property, which was then redistributed among their
former tenants. Some landlords were allowed to keep a portion of
their land and join the ranks of the peasantry, but the great majority
were subjected to public trial and denunciation by the local peasants.
The evidence that subsequently came to light suggested that as many
as one million landlords were killed during this early period of the
PRC's land reforms. These measures were the prelude to the later
wholesale collectivisation of the peasantry.

On the political front, it was not long before Mao and the CCP
began to resort to terror tactics. It soon became clear that China was
to be turned into a one-party state. At the time of the Communist
success in 1949 there had been over ten identifiable political parties

A landlord is humiliated by his former tenants, 1949

in China. These included the Left GMD and the Democratic League, splinter parties which had broken away from Chiang Kaishek's Nationalists. By 1952 they had disappeared, destroyed in a set of repressive moves which denied the right of political organisation to any but the CCP. The political purges were accompanied by a series of mass campaigns aimed at extending the CCP's control over the people of China. A concerted attack was launched against 'counter revolutionaries and imperialists', catch-all terms that were used to condemn anyone who showed signs of disapproving of the Communist regime.

The methods used to flush out such backsliders became the basic system for maintaining CCP control in China. Local Party workers encouraged neighbour to spy on neighbour, workers to inform on their fellows and children to report on their parents. This had the effect of forcibly politicising the nation. Individuals or families who declined to become involved were immediately labelled as class enemies. Indeed, 'labelling' became the chief means of enforcing obedience. Those Chinese who had a middle-class or non-revolutionary background knew that this would be sufficient to condemn them. To prove the sincerity of their acceptance of the new proletarian China they became avid in their readiness to denounce others as 'bourgeois elements' and 'imperialist lackeys'. In the People's Republic there was to be no toleration of detachment, let alone dissent. China had begun to take its first steps towards becoming a society of informers in which conformity was maintained by exploiting the traditional fear Chinese people had of being publicly exposed as political or social deviants.

Particular CCP severity was evident in Shanghai and Guangzhou (Canton), cities which had been notorious for their underworld gangs and triads in the years of Nationalist rule. Having used the local knowledge of the former gangsters to consolidate its hold on the city, the CCP turned on them in a violent bloodletting. Of the 130,000 'bandits and criminals' rounded up by the authorities in Guangzhou over half were executed. A similar process led to a death toll of 28,000 in Shanghai. As part of the CCP's coercion of China, youth organisations were either closed down or taken over by party cadres. Religion came under particular attack; Christian churches were forcibly closed, their property seized or destroyed and their ministers physically abused. Foreign priests and nuns were expelled from China. Wall posters, the traditional way by which Chinese governments disseminated their propaganda, and loud speakers at every corner kept up a running condemnation of religion. Confucianism, Buddhism and Christianity were denounced as worthless superstitions that had no place in the new nation. Slogans proclaiming the virtues of Maoist China were to be seen everywhere. China, possibly even more than the USSR, became a slogan-ridden society. The slogans became more than simply a way of exhorting the comrades to ever greater efforts;

they were a means of enforcing solidarity and conformity.

The repression imposed on the nation at this stage has to be understood in relation to two developments that dominated the early years of the PRC: the Korean War (1950-53) and Mao's First Five-Year Plan (1952-56). The Korean struggle (see pages 88-90) placed huge additional burdens on the young Communist Republic and was used to justify the extension of state control. The same applied to the industrialisation programme on which China embarked. Mao claimed that many officials were only half-hearted in their efforts to implement it. He identified two major culprits, Gao Gang (Kao Kang), a Central Council vice-chairman and the CCP leader in Manchuria, and Rao Rashi (Jao Shu-shih), who held the equivalent post in Shandong province. Mao asserted in 1954 that these two men, rather than working to advance China's industrialisation, had misused their authority to establish 'independent kingdoms'. Mao's charges were enough to lead to the Central Council's dismissal of both men. Gao Gang committed suicide, an act described by Deng Xiaoping, who along with Liu Shaoqi had been highly active in hounding him, as 'the ultimate treason'.

The high party status and reputation that Gao and Rao had enjoyed made their sudden fall all the more remarkable. It was clear evidence of the increasing centralisation of power in the Party and government and of Mao's refusal to tolerate the emergence of potential rivals. Notwithstanding the apparent harmony that the CCP leaders publicly displayed, tensions and rivalries were never far below the surface. The godlike status that Mao achieved among the Chinese people between 1949 and his death in 1976 did not make him more trustful of his colleagues. Indeed, his suspicions increased to the point of paranoia. A fact stressed by many biographers is that as Mao became more powerful he became increasingly detached from his political and governmental associates. Such was the awe in which he was held that his colleagues did not find it easy to converse or to exchange ideas with him and it is doubtful that they ever gave him their honest opinions. While it is true that Mao made a point in the 1950s of 'going to the people', his travels within China were largely stage-managed affairs. His claim that such journeys brought him in touch with the real feelings of the people is unconvincing; those peasants and workers who were selected for the privilege of speaking to him were coached into telling him only what he wanted to hear.

2 The Economy - The First Five-Year Plan, 1952-6

Mao's early attempts to modernise the Chinese economy carried the stamp of Soviet influence. Impressed by the apparent success of Stalin's series of five-year Plans in the USSR, Mao wanted the PRC to build on the same model. The emphasis would be on state-directed growth of heavy industry. A partial basis for this already existed. The

GMD government had established a National Resources Committee (NRC) which had taken control of industrial investment policy. A large number of the NRC's managers and over 200,000 of its work force had stayed on in China after 1949. In addition, a significant population shift had begun with the coming to power of the CCP. Between 1949 and 1957 migration from the countryside to the towns nearly doubled the urban population from fifty-seven million to one hundred million.

Thus as the PRC began its economic reforms it already had available a large potential workforce and considerable industrial expertise. However, the new government's first notable success was scored unaided. In its first two years it brought under control the galloping inflation from which China had suffered during the last years of the GMD. From a rate of 1,000 per cent in 1949 inflation had dropped to a manageable 15 per cent by 1951. This was largely achieved by slashing public expenditure, raising tax rates on urban dwellers, and replacing the old Chinese dollar with a new currency, known as the renminbi or yuan.

Under the PRC's first Five-Year Plan the areas targeted for increased production were coal, steel, and petro-chemicals. Attention was also to be given to the development of a Chinese automobile and transport industry. To boost morale a number of spectacular civil-engineering projects were undertaken. An outstanding example was the construction of a vast road and rail bridge across the Yangzi at Nanjing (Nanking). The degree of success thought to have been achieved by the Plan can be gauged from the following table:

The First Five-Year Plan, 1952-6

	Original Output Targets in 1952	Output Actually Achieved by 1957
Gross Industrial Output (value in millions of yuan)	53,560	65,020
Coal (million metric tonnes)	113	115
Oil (mmt)	2,012	1,458
Steel (mmt)	4.12	5.35
Electric power (billion kwh)	15.9	19.34
Hydro-electric turbines (kw)	79,000	74,900
Machine tools (units)	12,720	28,000
Locomotives (units)	200	167
Freight cars (units)	8,500	7,300
Merchant Ships (thousand tonnes)	179.15	54
Trucks (units)	4,000	7,500
Bicycles (units)	550,000	1,174,000
Manufactured chemicals (thousand metric tonnes)	1,580	2,087

It should be said that these statistics need to be regarded with caution. As in the USSR, so in the PRC, there was a tendency for officials to massage the figures relating to economic performance. All those in the spiral of command from CCP functionaries and industrial managers down to foremen and workers were anxious to appear to be fulfilling their targets. The presence of Party cadres checking on production targets meant that in many areas of industry there was what amounted to a large-scale conspiracy to adjust the figures so that they appeared as impressive as possible. Yet even allowing for exaggeration, the fact remained that the Plan had achieved a considerable degree of success in stimulating production, this moreover, at a time when the Korean War had forced China to finance a major war effort.

PRC Expenditure in Percentages of Total Budget			
	1950	1952	1957
Economic Development	25.5	45.4	51.4
Education and Culture	11.1	13.6	16.0
Defence	41.5	26.0	19.0
Government Administration	9.3	10.3	7.8
Miscellaneous	2.6	4.7	5.8
Total in millions of yuans	6,810	16,790	29,020

China's economic growth rate of nearly 9 per cent between 1953 and 1957 compared favourably with that of the USSR in the 1930s. In the circumstances of the 1950s it was natural that China should measure itself against the yardstick of the Soviet Union's industrial performance and seek to emulate its perceived success. At this stage Stalin's USSR was the PRC's political and economic mentor. It was, after all, the only country after the 1949 Revolution which was willing to offer China economic aid. Yet this aid was to prove a mixed blessing. In the Sino-Soviet agreement of 1950 (see page 114) the USSR agreed to provide China with economic assistance, but the bargain was weighted very much in favour of the Soviet Union. Soviet aid was not a fraternal gift; it had to be paid for by commercial concessions. For example, the PRC was required to send a substantial portion of its bullion reserves to the USSR. Furthermore, the 10,000 Soviet economic advisers who came to China came at a price. The PRC had to meet their costs by taking out high interest loans. Such loans were the predominant form of Soviet aid to China. Only 5 per cent of the capital sent to China was genuine industrial investment; the rest was in the form of loans. The realisation by the Chinese that they had been exploited rather than aided was a major factor in the later souring of Sino-Soviet relations.

3 The Hundred Flowers Campaign, 1957

Mao travelled extensively in China during the early 1950s. The rapturous reception he received wherever he went convinced him that he was in touch with the people. He informed his government and party colleagues that it was now appropriate to allow greater freedom of expression to those who might wish to comment constructively on how well Communist China was achieving its aim of transforming itself into a proletarian state. In a widely-reported speech on 'Contradictions', given to leading party workers early in 1957, Mao stated his satisfaction with the economic progress China was making, but went on to complain of the heavy-handedness with which CCP officials applied national and local policies. He hinted that the time might have come to allow intellectuals a greater say in debate. This was an unusual twist since Mao's abiding attitude towards intellectuals was one of distaste; he tended to regard them as parasitic idlers in a workers' state. But he had been sufficiently tolerant in 1956 not to give his backing to a campaign against the writer Hu Feng. Hu had dared to challenge the notion that Marxist-Leninist values were the sole criterion for judging artistic merit. His argument had brought bitter denunciations from the upper ranks of the CCP. However, Mao joined Zhou Enlai in suggesting that China had made such progress under the First Five-Year Plan that it could afford to be lenient towards Hu, confused and mistaken though he was.

Subsequent events suggested that Mao's apparent mellowing was an act. He had not really become more tolerant; he was engaged in a ruse. His aim was to appear to be adopting a moderate approach in order to lull critics within the CCP into thinking it was now safe to air their criticisms. Once they had revealed themselves they could then be denounced as anti-Party. In this way the CCP could be cleansed of those who were less than committed to its absolute authority.

Early in 1957 Mao urged Communist Party officials to be prepared to undergo criticism from the people. With the admonition, 'Let a hundred flowers bloom, let a hundred schools of thought contend', he called upon critics of the Party to specify their objections. Once they had overcome their initial fear of exposing themselves as being anti-party, members rushed to respond. A movement gathered momentum. Individuals and policies were attacked on the grounds of corruption, inefficiency and lack of realism. Leading figures in government, education and the arts were heavily censured for their failures. Things even went so far as to include mild criticism of Mao Zedong himself.

This was too much for Mao. He immediately called a halt to the campaign. Everything went into reverse; it became a time not of freedom of expression but of fierce repression. The Hundred Flowers campaign was abandoned and replaced by an 'anti-rightist' movement. Those who had been foremost in responding to Mao's call to let a hundred schools of thought contend were now forced to retract their statements. University staff and school teachers, research scientists, economists, writers and artists - many of the best minds and the most able public servants in China - were obliged to make abject confessions and submit themselves to 're-education'. The Party was purged of those members who had been too free with their objections to government and party orders.

The speed with which Mao had reversed his policy gives support to the view that, far from being a liberalising measure, the Hundred Flowers campaign had been a deliberate manoeuvre on his part to bring his critics into the open, the easier to identify and remove them. It was part of the movement towards a controlled society in which all expression, whether political or artistic, had to meet the criteria of political correctness as defined by Mao. The anti-rightist movement by which he purged the government and Party of his critics was of a scale and ruthlessness that anticipated the upheavals of the Cultural Revolution a decade later.

4 The Great Leap Forward, 1958-62

a) The Collectivisation of the Peasantry

The land policy adopted by Mao Zedong has to be seen as a complement to his industrialisation plans. Although he had come to power as leader of a great peasant revolution, he did not allow this to dictate his economic strategy. In his plans for the modernisation of China the industrialisation programme had priority over all other considerations. By the mid-1950s the organisers of the First Five-Year Plan had become aware that China had a severe labour shortage. Despite the migration from the land, those employed in industry still constituted a minority of the Chinese working population. The industrial workforce would have to be greatly increased if targets were to be met. It was further recognised that, although the peasants were undoubtedly producing more food, this was not finding its way to the urban workers. The common view among the economic planners was that this was the fault of the peasants: they were indulging themselves by over-eating and by having larger families which meant more mouths had to be fed. The authorities were convinced that the peasantry must be brought under strict central control and direction.

The PRC's initial land reforms had been introduced in the euphoria that had accompanied the 1949 Revolution. Land had been seized from the landlords and redistributed among the peasants. Yet even at that time the peasants had been urged to pool their resources by joining in farm collectives. This was the principle that was now forcibly extended. Between 1956 and 1958 the government directed that the existing 750,000 co-operatives be amalgamated into a number of large communes. In 1958 Mao made this collectivisation process an essential part of the Second Five-Year Plan (1958-62), better known, by the term he gave it, as 'The Great Leap Forward'. China's agricultural land was divided into 70,000 communes. Each commune was made up of roughly 750,000 brigades, each brigade containing some 200 households. The whole system was under the direct control of PRC's central government; farming methods, the sale and distribution of produce, and the setting of prices were to be dictated from above. Private farming would cease to exist.

It has been suggested that Mao's ideas sprang from a belief he shared with Stalin that the peasant left to himself was 'inherently capitalistic'. John King Fairbank, the American expert on modern China, remarked on the paradox of collectivisation: 'the revolutionary state, having established its legitimacy by freeing the peasant from landlordism and other constraints, now had him boxed in as never before. The state had become the ultimate landlord'. In public Mao maintained that collectivisation, far from being forced on the peasants, was a direct response to their wishes. In the summer of 1958 the CCP's Central Committee made the following declaration in Mao's name:

1 The people have taken to organizing themselves along military lines, working with militancy, and leading a collective life, and this has raised the political consciousness of the 500 million peasants still further. Community dining rooms, kindergartens, nurseries, sewing groups,
5 barber shops, public baths, happy homes for the aged, agricultural middle schools, "red and expert" schools, are leading the peasants toward a happier collective life and further fostering ideas of collectivism among the peasant masses ...
   In the present circumstances, the establishment of people's
10 communes with all-round management of agriculture, forestry, animal husbandry, side occupations, and fishery, where industry (the worker), agriculture (the peasant), exchange (the trader), culture and education (the student), and military affairs (the militiaman) merge into one, is the fundamental policy to guide the peasants to accel-
15 erate socialist construction, complete the building of socialism ahead of time, and carry out the gradual transition to communism.

b) The Famine

The collectivisation programme that was begun in 1958 entailed a vast social transformation which resulted in the greatest famine in Chinese history. The disruption caused by the ending of private farming was a major cause of hunger since it discouraged the individual peasant from producing food beyond his own immediate needs. But that was only part of the story. Equally significant was Mao's belief that Chinese agronomists had made a series of discoveries about crop growing that would revolutionise food production. Chinese scientists were in thrall to Trofim Lysenko, the Soviet researcher whom Stalin regarded as the voice of scientific truth. It was later realised and admitted that Lysenko's ideas were worthless. Indeed, it was already known in the USSR that Lysenko's theories about producing 'super-crops' had proved wholly fraudulent and had contributed to the Soviet famines of the 1930s. But such was the influence of the USSR in the early years of the PRC that the Chinese regarded Lysenko as infallible. A generation of Chinese researchers were trained in the notion that he could do no wrong. A Beijing doctor recorded: 'We were told that the Soviets had discovered and invented everything, even the aeroplane. We had to change textbooks and rename things in Lysenko's honour'. Mao made Lysenkoism official policy in 1958 when he personally drafted an eight-point agricultural 'constitution' based on the theories of crop growth advanced by Lysenko and his Chinese disciples, which farmers were forced to follow. The eight headings were:

1   The popularisation of new breeds and seeds
2   Close planting
3   Deep ploughing
4   Increased fertilisation
5   The innovation of farm tools
6   Improved field management
7   Pest control
8   Increased irrigation

Whatever merit these injunctions might have had if selectively applied was destroyed by the demand that they be universally enforced. The most graphic instance of the tragic results that followed from unthinking application was in regard to pest control. The whole Chinese population was called upon to end the menace of sparrows and other wild birds which ate crop seeds. So, at designated times, the Chinese came out from their houses and with any implement they could lay their hands on made as much noise as possible. Clanging plates, metal pots and pans, they kept up a continuous din that prevented the birds from landing, so that they eventually dropped exhausted from the sky. The thousands of dead birds were then publicly displayed as trophies. The outcome was catastrophic. With no birds now to thin their numbers, insects and small creatures multiplied prodigiously and gorged themselves on the grains and plants. The larger birds that would have fed off the smaller were no longer around to prey on rats and their kind. Vermin multiplied and destroyed stocks of grain. The absurdity of the enterprise became only too evident in the hunger that it caused, but nobody dared say a critical word since to have done so would have been to challenge Mao's wisdom.

The bewildered local peasant communities, their way of life already dislocated by collectivisation, proved incapable of adapting to the threat of famine. Constrained by the state regulations imposed from on high, many areas became defeatist in the face of impending doom. Those peasants who showed initiative by trying to circumvent the new laws and return to their old ways of production risked severe punishment. Chinese prisons and penal colonies were expanded to incarcerate the great numbers of starving peasants who fell foul of the authorities. In these camps, the equivalent of the Soviet gulag prison system, hundreds of thousands, possibly millions, starved to death.

It was certainly the case that millions died in the countryside. Hunger was not unknown in the urban areas but it was in the rural provinces of China that the famine was at its worst. Henan (Honan) and Anhui (Anhwei) were particularly badly affected. Gansu (Kansu), Sichuan (Szechwan), Hebei (Hopei) and Xinjiang (Sinkiang) were other areas that experienced appalling suffering. Parents sold their children and husbands sold their wives for food. Women prostituted themselves to obtain food for their families, and there were many instances of peasants offering themselves as slaves to anyone who would feed them. The following account of cannibalism in Liaoning province is typical of the experiences that later came to light:

1 A peasant woman, unable to stand the incessant crying for food of her two-year-old daughter, and thinking perhaps to end her suffering, had strangled her. She had given the girl's body to her husband, asking him to bury it. Instead, out of his mind with hunger, he put the body in the
5 cooking pot with what little food they had foraged. He had forced his wife to eat a bowl of the resulting stew. His wife, in a fit of remorse, had reported her husband's crime to the authorities. The fact that she came forward voluntarily made no difference. Although there was no law against cannibalism in the criminal code of the People's Republic,
10 the Ministry of Public Security treated such cases, which were all too common, with the utmost severity. Both husband and wife were arrested and summarily executed.

Arguably, it was Tibet that experienced the greatest degree of misery; 20 per cent of its population was wiped out by starvation. In Qinghai (Tsinghai) province, the birthplace of the Dalai Lama, over half the population died from hunger. It was a tragedy that the Panchen Lama described in 1962 as a deliberate act of genocide. Had the grip of the central government not been so tight the desperation of these provinces might well have produced civil war. What deepened the tragedy was that many government advisers were fully aware of the facts. They knew that Lysenkoism was nonsense and that people were dying by the million, but they dared not speak out. Indeed, the reverse happened; Party cadres and officials reported back to Beijing that production targets were being met and that the Great Leap Forward was on course. Sir Percy Craddock, British Ambassador in China in the 1960s, commented:

1 Sycophantic provincial leaders cooked the books; immense increases, two or three fold, were reported; and, in obedience to the bogus figures, an impoverished province such as Anhui delivered grain it desperately needed itself to the state, or even for export abroad as

5   surplus. On his inspection tours Mao saw the close-planted fields that
     he wanted to see; the local officials moved in extra shoots from other
     fields and moved them back when he had gone.

It was rarely that a person of note would admit what was really
happening. When Peng Dehuai (Peng Teh-huai), the Minister of
Defence, dared to do so at a Party gathering in Lushan in 1959 he was
denounced by his fellow ministers and dismissed. But eventually, such
was the scale of China's wretchedness, the truth came out. Even Mao
himself accepted it. But his reaction was characteristic. Rather than
acknowledge that his own ideas had contributed to the disaster, he
rounded on his officials, accusing them of incompetence. Yet no
matter how culpable those lower down in the Communist hierarchy
may have been, the responsibility lay with Mao Zedong. It was in
pursuit of his instructions regarding the restructuring of the Chinese
peasantry and in accordance with his mistaken notions of science that
his officials had set in motion a process that culminated in the
horrific deaths of thirty million Chinese.

China's Agricultural Record, 1952-62			
Year	Grain Production (millions tonnes)	Meat Production (millions tonnes)	Index of Gross Output Value of Agriculture
1952	163.9	3.4	100.0
1953	166.8	3.8	103.1
1954	169.5	3.9	106.6
1955	183.9	3.3	114.7
1956	192.8	3.4	120.5
1957	195.1	4.0	124.8
1958	200.0	4.3	127.8
1959	170.0	2.6	110.4
1960	143.5	1.3	96.4
1961	147.5	1.2	94.1
1962	160.0	1.9	99.9

c) Industry

Such was the scale of the famine of the late 1950s and early 1960s that
it has tended to overshadow analyses of the Great Leap Forward.
However, at the time agriculture was very much a secondary concern
for Mao; it was industrialisation that mattered. He resolved to achieve
industrial 'lift-off' for China by harnessing what he regarded as the
nation's greatest resource - its massive population. Mao's belief was
that the Chinese people could, with their own hands, create a modern
industrial economy, powerful enough to compete with the capitalist
West. The classic expression of this was Mao's insistence on 'backyard

furnaces'; China would draw its supplies of iron and steel not from large foundries and steel mills but from primitive smelting devices that every family was encouraged to build on its premises. Here was a communal activity in which all the Chinese could participate, conscious that by their own efforts they were helping to build the new society.

Mao, like Stalin, was greatly impressed by the grand project. Size mattered. It was the scale of a construction rather than its economic value which appealed to him. He was convinced that by sheer manpower China could solve all the problems of industrial development. It is true that prodigious feats were achieved by the force of manual labour. Mechanical diggers were shunned in favour of the earth being moved by the hands of the workers. Giant span bridges, canals and dams were constructed. These were lauded by the CCP as the visible proof of China's resurgence under Communism. The building of Tiananmen Square in Beijing was begun in 1957 and completed within two years. This was an enormous project that involved clearing a hundred-acre site of its teeming homes, shops and markets and laying a vast concrete-paved level space, open to the south, but with two huge new buildings to the east and west and the Forbidden City to the north.

But while such feats thrilled the Chinese and impressed foreigners, the Plan as a whole did not reach its objectives. It did not succeed because it ignored basic economics. Mass labour does not necessarily result in mass production. Avoiding the sophisticated industrial techniques of the decadent West may have met the demands of revolutionary ideology but it did not make economic sense. Enthusiasm was not enough. Good will did not produce good steel. Both in the quantity of its raw materials and the quality of its finished products, China, under the Great Leap Forward, fell a long way short of meeting its domestic industrial requirements. The notion of its being internationally competitive was wildly unrealistic.

The common belief in the CCP was that applied Communism would always produce an effective system of production and fair shares for all. When it did not, Mao interpreted the lack of achievement not as a failure of Communism itself, but as the result of sabotage by bourgeois elements and backsliders. His invariable response to the news of failure was to blame the messenger. The first stage was to deny the bad results and then, when they could no longer be disputed, to search for the culprits responsible for administering the policies wrongly, either through incompetence or deliberate sabotage. It is extraordinary how so much of what passed for planning was really only a set of politically inspired slogans. The reports of the party conferences called to deal with particular failures describe the delegates shouting slogans and counter-slogans at each other instead of addressing the real economic problems.

Although the record of the Great Leap Forward is largely a study in failure there was an outstanding scientific success that China could celebrate - its development as a nuclear power. The research programme which eventually led to the detonation of an atomic bomb in 1964 and a hydrogen bomb in 1967 was initiated in the late 1950s largely in response to the rift in Sino-Soviet relations which convinced Mao that China must develop as a unilateral nuclear power.

China's Economic Performance, 1952-62			
Year	Index of National Income	Growth of National Income (%)	Inflation
1952	100.0		-0.4
1953	114.0	14.0	3.4
1954	120.6	5.8	2.3
1955	128.3	6.4	1.0
1956	146.4	14.1	0
1957	153.0	4.5	1.5
1958	186.7	22.0	0.2
1959	202.1	8.2	0.9
1960	199.2	-1.4	3.1
1961	140.0	-29.7	16.2
1962	130.9	-6.5	3.8

5 The Power Struggle, 1961-6

By 1961 it was evident that not only had the Great Leap Forward failed to meet its industrial targets, but also that its agrarian policies had caused catastrophe. Mao's reputation within the Party had undoubtedly been damaged. In 1962 , therefore, he called upon President Liu Shaoqi and CCP General Secretary Deng Xiaoping to take personal responsibility for ending the chaos on the land and restoring adequate food supplies.

In attempting to tackle the problem Liu and Deng enlisted the aid of Chen Yun, acknowledged as the CCP's leading economic theorist. Together they concluded that the only immediate solution to the food crisis was to allow markets to operate again, thereby providing individual farmers with an incentive to produce surplus stocks. This was a tacit admission that the commune system had been a failure. Mao became uneasy with the methods adopted by Liu and Deng; if they considered that the only path to a successful recovery was by giving precedence to purely economic considerations this would undermine the collectivist principle on which he had set such store as a social revolutionary.

Mao was further concerned by an accompanying political threat - the increased popularity of Liu and Deng within the Party. Mao never lost his fear that his colleagues, even those who professed the greatest personal loyalty, were ready to remove him from power should the opportunity arise. Mao judged that Liu and Deng were using their position to mount a challenge. He had grounds for his suspicions; in Gansu and Qinghai provinces in the early 1960s supporters of Liu, Deng and Chen Yun took over the local government and began to reverse the collectivisation programme. Many of the details of what happened in the localities remain unclear but the majority of the provincial leaders appear to have remained loyal to Mao. Nevertheless, Mao judged that he was losing his grip on the Party and that a power struggle was looming. He regretted having given up the Presidency of the PRC in 1958; although he had retained his Chairmanship of the CCP, his voluntary restricting of his own authority had, he felt, encouraged the growth of opposition. He also judged that it had been an error to have largely abandoned his regular public appearances after 1958. His withdrawal from the political scene had enabled factions to develop. It was to reverse this trend and regain his dominance that Mao turned to Lin Biao (Lin Piao). A dedicated Maoist, Lin was a Marshal of the PLA and had been Defence Minister since 1959. His reverence for Mao and his leadership of the PLA made him an invaluable ally.

It was Lin Biao who in the early 1960s collaborated with Chen Boda (Chen Po-ta), the editor of the CCP journal, *Red Flag*, in compiling 'the Little Red Book'. Formally entitled *Quotations from Chairman Mao Zedong*, the book was a collection of the thoughts and sayings of Mao since the 1920s. Its thirty-three chapters covered such topics as 'The Communist Party', 'Classes and Class Struggle', and 'Culture and Art'. The work was prefaced by Lin Biao's exhortation: 'Study Chairman Mao's writings, follow his teachings and act according to his instructions'. Lin made the Little Red Book, the secular bible of China, the source of all truth. A copy was distributed to every soldier and became the basic text used in the study sessions which were a compulsory and daily part of military training. In this way the PLA, the institution with the highest prestige and proudest revolutionary tradition in Communist China, was politicised as a force totally committed to the support of Mao Zedong. This soon carried over into the civilian sphere. Mao's slogan 'learn from the PLA' carried the clear message that China's army represented the true revolutionary spirit and was therefore the model for the people to emulate. The Little Red Book became the prescribed source for every subject on the curriculum in the schools and universities. In shops and factories, workers began their day and filled their breaks with communal readings from it. Throughout China it became necessary to have a copy of *Quotations from Chairman Mao Zedong* with one at all times; it was the required text, used to define all issues and settle all arguments.

The Maoist propaganda campaign made further ground with the publication in 1963 of *The Diary of Lei Feng*. This book purported to be the daily journal of a humble PLA lorry driver whose every thought and action were inspired by his devotion to Mao. The manner in which Lei died, accidentally crushed under the wheels of a truck while faithfully performing his assigned duties, was held up as a symbol of martyrdom for the revolutionary cause. That the story was a total fabrication did not prevent its hero from achieving secular sainthood. Lei Feng was extolled by Maoists as the embodiment of the loyalty of the ordinary Chinese, a loyalty that by implication stood in marked contrast to the time-serving careerism of many in the CCP. Lei Feng's *Diary* joined the Little Red Book as an essential text for study in China's schools.

The central importance of literary and cultural works in the mounting power struggle was especially evident in the furore that developed over a play, *The Dismissal of Hai Rai from Office*, written by Wu Han. This work, performed between 1961 and 1965, was set in the days of the Song dynasty (AD 960-1279) and had as its theme the defiance of a corrupt government by a courageous official. The title referred to the wrongful dismissal of Hai Rai by a tyrannical ruler. Since Wu Han belonged to a group of writers who were critical of Mao Zedong, it was possible to interpret his play as a condemnation of Mao's previous dismissal of Marshal Peng Dehuai for opposing the Great Leap Forward. The pro-Maoists awoke to the import of the play in 1965 and launched a series of attacks on Wu, charging him with besmirching Mao's good name and undermining Marxism-Leninism.

The Wu Han affair further polarised the divisions within the CCP and between the CCP and PLA. It thus provided Lin Biao with added justification for moving against the anti-Maoist elements in the Communist Party. It was at this stage that Mao's wife, Jiang Qing, a former bit-part film actress in Shanghai, began to play a prominent role. As the Chairman's spouse she had an influence that was dangerous to challenge. A fierce hard-liner, Jiang denounced the 'reactionaries and revisionists' on the right of the Party. She also aimed to undermine the Group of Five, a representative set of professional party bureaucrats led by Peng Zhen (Peng Chen), the mayor of Beijing, whose essential objective was to act as conciliators to prevent party splits widening. Despite their declared loyalty to Mao, the Group of Five were condemned by Jiang for their moderation at a time when utter ruthlessness was the only proper response. As leader of a rival group of leftist radicals, 'the Shanghai Forum', Jiang urged that steps be immediately taken to remove Liu Shaoqi and Deng Xiaoping from their positions in the CCP. She further demanded that Chinese culture be cleansed of those writers and artists whose attitude betrayed their lack of commitment to Mao's revolution. The severity of her approach led Lin Biao to ask her to take responsibility for overseeing the PLA's cultural policy.

What was at issue was no longer merely a political question. Jiang was working towards the establishment of a new Chinese culture which would reject the past and conform totally to the socialist ideas of Mao Zedong. Asserting that the thoughts of Chairman Mao represented a 'new development of the Marxist-Leninist world outlook', the Shanghai Forum identified the counter-revolutionaries who must be struggled against and destroyed.

1 China is under the dictatorship of a sinister anti-Party and anti-Socialist line which is diametrically opposed to Chairman Mao's thought. This sinister line is a combination of bourgeois ideas on literature and art, modern revisionist ideas on literature and art and what is known as the literature and art of the 1930s.

The answer was for the PLA, 'the mainstay and hope of the Chinese people', to lead China in rooting out 'anti-socialist weeds' and eradicating all traces of artistic corruption that delayed the achievement of a truly proletarian culture. Lin Biao spoke of an 'imminent and inevitable' struggle against class enemies. This proved to be the prelude to a purge of the Party, which began as an attack by Mao on those he defined as 'taking the capitalist road'. Intermixed with the declared intention of purifying China was the settling of old scores and the removal of rivals. In April 1966 Peng Zhen and the leading members of the Group of Five were denounced, as was the playwright Wu Han. The ground had been prepared by Maoists packing the key Party committees; especially significant was the Maoist control of the Central Cultural Revolution Committee, a sub-committee of the Politburo. By the summer of 1966 Liu Shaoqi and Deng Xiaoping found themselves being outmanoeuvred and undermined. China was about to enter that tumultuous and terrifying period of political and social history known as 'the Cultural Revolution'.

Summary Diagram
China Under Mao: Politics and Economics, 1949-66

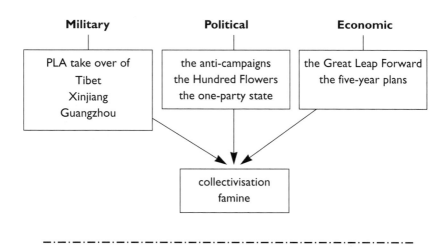

Consolidation and Control

Military

PLA take over of
Tibet
Xinjiang
Guangzhou

Political

the anti-campaigns
the Hundred Flowers
the one-party state

Economic

the Great Leap Forward
the five-year plans

collectivisation
famine

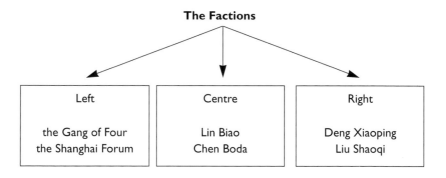

The Contenders for Power 1961-6

The Factions

Left

the Gang of Four
the Shanghai Forum

Centre

Lin Biao
Chen Boda

Right

Deng Xiaoping
Liu Shaoqi

3 China Under Mao: The Cultural Revolution, 1966-76

On 18 August 1966 an extraordinary event took place in Beijing. Over a million people, the majority of them in their teens or early twenties, packed into Tiananmen Square. Waving their Little Red Books, they screamed themselves hoarse in an impassioned outpouring of veneration for their idol, Chairman Mao. This massive demonstration was the first event in the Cultural Revolution, a movement that aimed at nothing less than the creation of a new type of Chinese society and which was to convulse the whole of China for the next decade. Mao had enlisted the youth of China as his instrument for reimposing his will upon the nation and reshaping it according to his vision.

Mao identified 'four olds' as targets for the young to attack - old culture, old thoughts, old customs and old habits. There is a striking irony in a man of seventy-three appealing to the young to overthrow the old, but at the time it went unnoticed by the youngsters. As 'Red Guards', they rushed to do his bidding with a terrifying intensity and ferocity. It is doubtful whether any other society has witnessed organised upheaval on such a scale. Hardly anywhere in China, even the remotest regions, remained untouched. There was scarcely a family unaffected by what happened. Millions died; many more millions had their lives irreparably damaged.

1 Mao's Purpose in Launching the Cultural Revolution

An obvious question arises. Why was Mao Zedong willing to plunge into renewed turmoil a nation which had only just emerged from decades of foreign occupation, civil war and famine? At its simplest, the answer is that the Cultural Revolution was to be the means by which Mao would reassert his authority over China and the CCP. He had two principal objectives: to preserve himself in power for the rest of his life and to ensure that his concept of revolution would continue after his death. Mao believed that the revolution was in danger of being betrayed from within; he was convinced that many in the upper echelons of the CCP were infected by 'neo-capitalism' and a desire for personal power that robbed them of their revolutionary purpose.

The Great Proletarian Cultural Revolution, to give it its full title, has, therefore, to be seen as an extension of Mao's belief in permanent revolution, his conviction that revolution was not a historical event but a continuing process. He believed that if the Chinese revolution stood still it would cease to be a genuine revolution, and he feared that after him the CCP would simply become a self-justifying bureaucracy which would destroy all that had been achieved by the PRC since 1949. To prevent this he planned to circumvent the party bureaucracy and appeal directly to the Chinese people. In a great populist gesture he would enlist them in a campaign to save and consolidate the revolution. Mao used a memorable paradox to describe his policy; he spoke of 'great disorder across the land leading to great order'; only by a policy of deliberate disruption could the forces of reaction be exposed and destroyed.

Mao had also been disturbed by developments in the USSR, China's great Communist rival. In the late 1950s he had interpreted the retrospective Soviet attack upon Stalin's 'cult of personality' as a criticism of his own leadership of China. The news in 1964 of the fall from power of the Soviet leader, Nikita Khrushchev, gave Mao further concern. The official reason given by the Soviet authorities for their dismissal of Khrushchev was that he had engaged in 'harebrained' economic schemes. Nobody in China had openly dared to use such a term in regard to Mao's policies, but the parallel between the political situations in the USSR and China was too close for comfort.

Mao's anxieties went beyond the purely personal. What he observed in the Soviet Union was a party, originally pure in revolutionary spirit, corrupted by its own exercise of power into a self-perpetuating elite. Despite his many personal differences with Stalin, Mao had never been willing to accept the lengths to which de-Stalinisation and liberalising had gone in the USSR. He viewed Khrushchev and his successors as guilty of betraying the revolution by encouraging revisionism and by detente with the West. Mao was determined that such developments would not happen in China after him. He judged that CCP and government officials were already being seduced by the privileges of power. He had convinced himself that the older revolutionaries who had defeated the Nationalists and established the People's Republic had lost their revolutionary fervour. Consequently, the only way to save his revolution was by waging war against the Communist Party hierarchy itself. It was a time for a new generation of Party members to replace the old guard.

However, Mao also judged that the younger members of the Party had yet to be tested. They had not undergone the legendary experiences of the CCP - the White Terror, the Long March, the anti-Japanese war, and the struggle against the GMD. They needed hardening in the crucible of revolutionary struggle. Only then would it be certain that they were strong enough to withstand a concerted military attack from the West, an eventuality in which Mao continued to believe throughout the 1960s. Here another striking parallel between Mao and Stalin presents itself. The most powerful motivating influence on Stalin in foreign affairs had been his conviction that the capitalist powers were intent on attacking the USSR. Mao had a similar fear of a Western strike against China. The perceived threat was used by both leaders in their respective countries to justify the imposition of the strictest political and social control.

A complementary aim was Mao's determination to preserve the Chinese Revolution as an essentially peasant movement. He did not want affairs to be run by the bureaucrats and intellectuals in the cities. A tension had developed between Mao and the urban intelligentsia. It was they who had criticised the Great Leap Forward. As a practical revolutionary Mao had always distrusted intellectuals as being more interested in theory than in action. Some historians have interpreted his assault on them in the Cultural Revolution as an act of revenge on a class which had continued to despise him ever since his days as an assistant librarian at Beijing University. Roderick MacFarqhar argued that while Mao did not originally intend the Cultural Revolution as an anti-intellectual vendetta, circumstances turned it into one:

1 I don't know that he was deliberately trying to destroy the intellectual class, so much as trying to transform them and to make them less elitist, more aware of the trials and tribulations of ordinary workers and peasants. Very few Chinese at that time had a higher education and very few
5 people could be considered intellectuals and there was a sort of disdain on the part of intellectuals towards workers and peasants and I think there still is today, but I think what he was really attempting to do was to bring those disparate groups closer together, but the price of course was the terrible destruction of the intellectuals.

2 The Course of the Cultural Revolution - The First Phase

The Cultural Revolution broadened from an internal party purge to a public movement with a poster campaign in the summer of 1966. Mao encouraged students and radical teachers in the universities to put up wall posters attacking the education system for its divergence from the revolutionary path. The enthusiasm with which the students abandoned their classes and attacked their teachers caused such unrest that Deng Xiaoping and Liu Shaoqi sent special work teams to the campuses in an attempt to contain the trouble. Zhou Enlai, ever the diplomat, tried to keep the peace between the party factions, between those who wanted to restore order and the Maoist elements who were eager for the disruption to spread. But in an atmosphere of increasing violence even his best efforts were in vain. The work teams were attacked by the students who, in a particularly ominous development, began to take to the streets. Wearing red arm bands, supplied to them by Maoist officials, these 'Red Guards' began a reign of terror.

It was at this critical stage that Mao Zedong made a dramatic public reappearance. In July 1966 in a stage-managed extravaganza, he was seen swimming in the Yangzi River at Wuhan (Wu Chang), the scene of the 1911 Revolution. Photos of this feat filled the Chinese newspapers and television and cinema newsreels carried the pictures into every village. Whether it was really Mao in the water is uncertain. There have been suggestions that the swimmer was a Mao look-alike or that Mao was standing on a submerged platform or being supported by aqua-divers. But the truth was unimportant. What mattered was that Mao had made a great symbolic gesture that excited the whole of China. The seventy-three-year-old Chairman had proved that he was very much alive and, therefore, still in control of events. John King Fairbank has suggested that to understand the impact of the incident on the Chinese imagination one needs to think of the reaction there would be in Britain to 'the news that Queen Elizabeth II had swum the Channel'.

Mao exploited the adulation aroused by his spectacular return to tighten his grip on government and party. In August he summoned a special meeting of the Central Committee, at which he condemned the revisionist tendencies in the Party and called upon members to rededicate themselves to unwavering class struggle. Mao also announced the downgrading of Liu Shaoqi in the party ranking and the elevation of Lin Biao to second in command. This was in effect to nominate Lin as his successor. Lin responded by addressing the great Red Guard rallies held in Tiananmen Square in the same month. He called upon the massed crowds to honour Mao Zedong as the outstanding revolutionary genius of the age who was 'remoulding the souls of the people'. It was this attempt to remould the people of China that was to give the Cultural Revolution its chilling and deadly character.

At the August meeting of the Central Committee Chen Boda accused Deng and Liu of being 'the spearheads of the erroneous line'. But no immediate action was taken against them since it was reported that Mao was willing to give them the opportunity 'to correct their mistakes'. However, two months later, following a Red Guard demonstration in Beijing aimed specifically against them, Deng and Liu were both formally dismissed from their positions in government and party on the grounds that they had adopted 'a bourgeois reactionary line' and had become 'Soviet revisionists'. Mao let it be known that he had been offended by the way in which Deng and Liu had previously tried to bypass him. He complained that they had treated him 'like their dead parent at a funeral'.

Wall posters were displayed denouncing both men for their betrayal of Maoist thought. Liu was dragged from his government residence and subjected to a series of brutal 'struggle sessions' before being imprisoned in foul conditions which were deliberately intended to break his health. He eventually died in 1973 in solitary confinement, lying in his own excreta and denied any form of medical treatment. Deng Xiaoping's son, Pufang, was thrown from an upstairs window by Red Guards, an act of gratuitous violence that broke his spine and left him permanently paralysed. Deng himself suffered less harshly but he was forced to undergo public humiliation which involved his being ranted at by 3,000 Red Guards. He then disappeared into solitary confinement before being sent to perform 'corrective labour' in Jiangxi province in 1969.

The acquiescence by the CCP and the PLA in the dismissal of such prominent figures testified to the power that Lin Biao and Jiang Qing were able to exert in Mao's name. This authority was increased by the appointment of Kang Sheng as head of China's special security forces, the PRC's secret police. Kang, who had a reputation for ruthlessness dating back to the Yanan years, was a member of the Shanghai Forum and a devotee of Jiang Qing. He became a principal organiser of the purges that continued, ostensibly at Mao's bidding, to decimate the upper echelons of the CCP throughout 1966 and 1967.

Once it was underway, Mao played little part in directing the Cultural Revolution. He withdrew from Beijing to Hangzhou (Hangchow) in central China, leaving the officials at Zhongnanhai, the government complex off Tiananmen Square, to the mercy of the Red Guards. Camped outside in the Square for months on end, the Guards kept up a constant loudspeaker barrage of insults directed at ministers and officials deemed to be 'rightists'. Anyone trying to break cover and leave the blockaded offices had to run the gauntlet of jeering youngsters who were eager to turn their insults into blows if given the slightest pretext. Jiang Qing and Lin Biao made sure that the besiegers were kept informed by going down in person to identify the ministers and officials who were to be abused and intimidated.

3 The Red Guard Terror

The Red Guard movement grew out of prepared soil. Since the Sino-Soviet divide in the 1950s, pupils and students had been encouraged to regard themselves as pioneers under Mao Zedong in the advancement of international proletarian revolution. Mass rallies had been used in the Hundred Flowers and anti-rightist campaigns in the 1950s. A student recalled:

1 The revolutionary fervour was definitely very strong, I think, in the educational system starting from the split between the Russian and Chinese Communist Party. I think the students and learning classes became much more politicised, and the competition I won with my

5 essay was how to be successful in the revolution. I remember I had all the big rhetoric and empty slogans and everybody loved it. Some people cried and I was very proud. That was 1965, so the education was already gearing up to a very charged class struggle and preparation.

In choosing China's youth to be the instruments of the Cultural

Revolution Mao showed an astute grasp of mass psychology. The young were made to feel that they had a special role to play not only in the regeneration of the nation but in the creation of a new socialist world order:

1 Now it was our generation's turn to defend China. China was the only
   country which wasn't revisionist, capitalist or colonialist. We felt that we
   were defending China's revolution and liberating the world. All the big
   slogans made a generation of us feel that the Cultural Revolution really
5 was a war, a war to defend Chairman Mao and the new China.

The reminiscences of those who had been Red Guards illustrate the extraordinary hold Mao had over them:

1 When Chairman Mao waved his hand at Tiananmen, a million Red
   Guards wept their hearts out as if by some hormonal reaction. Later on
   we were all conditioned to burst into tears the moment he appeared
   on the screen. He was divine, and the revolutionary tides of the world
5 rose and fell at his command.

   I believed in Mao with every cell in my body. You felt you would give
   Chairman Mao your everything - your body, your mind, your spirit, your
   soul, your fate. Whatever Chairman Mao wanted you to do you were
   ready to do it. So we were all there crying and jumping up and down
10 and shouting ourselves hoarse.

   When you see the red flags and when you see how emotional everybody was you get carried away with that sort of feeling as well. You just
   think I should be part of that, I should belong to that because there are
   millions of people there and everybody loved and worshipped Mao so
15 much that you would question yourself if you didn't feel like that.

   I cut a small hole in my chest with a penknife and pinned my Mao
   badge there. That way I thought that when I put my clothes on no one
   would be able to see it and I would have Chairman Mao literally
   engraved on my heart.

The awe in which Mao was held by the young was extreme but it was not wholly irrational. It was a recognition of what he had achieved for China. The young persons who ecstatically chanted Mao's name saw him as the great hero who had freed China from a century of humiliation at the hands of the foreigner. One of the most popular titles given to him was 'the red sun rising in the east', an apt metaphor for the man who had made China a great world power, possessing its own nuclear weapons and capable of displacing the Soviet Union as leader of the international socialist movement. In a shrewd analysis, Anthony Grey, a British correspondent who was imprisoned by the Chinese during the Cultural Revolution, suggested that the veneration of Mao illustrated the persistence of two remarkable features of Chinese society - emperor worship and the power of conformity.

1   The most extravagant and ridiculous language was used all the time
about him in the official press and in the Red Guard newspapers. I
remember I saw him once on May Day just by the merest chance; I was
in a crowd in the park and I was talking to members of the crowd and
5   I was saying, 'What were you hoping to see?' they said 'Chairman Mao,
we love Chairman Mao'. And they really did say it in a way that made
me think of the tendency of young people who want something to
idolise, be it pop singers or film stars or in their case the only one
charismatic individual in a nation. He had managed to work a great spell
10   over the people. I think he used the old admiration for China's
emperors and the son of heaven idea which was very strong - inculcated
almost into the Chinese nature. He was an extraordinarily charismatic
figure and he exploited this for all it was worth.

Mao knew that the need to conform to the standards of their peers is
very powerful among the young and that this makes them particularly
susceptible to suggestion. The more idealistic they are, the more
easily led they are. As Anthony Grey hinted, this phenomenon is not
restricted to China. There are many examples in the West of the herd
instinct taking over from individualism. Peer-group conformity is the
explanation for the hold that fashion, in such areas as clothing and
music, has over many impressionable young people. Nor should
simple perversity be left out of the account. Marching through the
streets chanting slogans is a softer option than working at one's
studies.

Yet it was more serious than that. There was a terrifying and deadly
side to the Red Guard movement. The young were deliberately
brutalised. Mao's presentation of chaos as more virtuous than order
was tantamount to declaring that there was no moral restriction on
what could be done in the name of the revolution. Students, trained
in the Chinese tradition of obedience to parents and teachers, were
suddenly told to insult and abuse them. For children to denounce
their elders had enormous significance in a society where respect was
ingrained. In a reversal of their traditional deference they behaved
with a particular vehemence. They were, of course, still being
obedient, but this time to a new master.

Anything that represented the corrupt past was labelled under the
blanket term, 'Confucius and Co', and was liable to be smashed or
torn up. Temples, shrines, works of art and ornamental gardens
became obvious targets; many priceless and irreplaceable treasures of
Chinese civilisation were destroyed in this wave of organised
vandalism. In the words of a Western correspondent: 'Mao told the
Red Guards: "To rebel is justified!". They repaid him by crushing
almost every semblance of tradition, decency and intellectual
endeavour in China, save that of a few protected institutes, where
scientific and military-related work continued fitfully in dangerous
circumstances.'

Given free reign, the Red Guards seized public transport and took over radio and television networks. Anyone showing signs of 'decadent tendencies' - the most obvious examples being the wearing of Western clothes, jewellery or make up - was likely to be manhandled and publicly humiliated. An especially vulnerable group were the 'intellectuals' a term used loosely to denote all those whose way of life or work was deemed to detach them from the people. School teachers, university staff, writers, and even doctors were prey to the Red Guard squads who denounced them as 'bad elements' and made them publicly confess their class crimes. Those judged to be particularly culpable were forced to undergo 'struggle sessions'.

These ordeals, which became a dominant feature of the Cultural Revolution, were in essence an assault on the individual's sense of self and were aimed at provoking and stimulating guilt. 'Brainwashing' is an appropriate term to describe the terror tactics. To induce guilt the victims were made to study Maoist documents followed by periods of intense self-criticism and confession. The first confession was never accepted; the accused had to dig deeper and deeper into their memory to recall all their errors and sins against the Party and the people. A common practice was for the Guards to force the accused to adopt the 'aeroplane' posture; with head thrust down, knees bent and arms pulled high behind the back. Those who maintained their innocence were systematically punched and kicked. After days of torment and constant denunciation as 'imperialist dogs', 'lick-spittle capitalists', 'lackeys of the USA' and 'betrayers of the people', few had the physical or mental strength to continue resisting.

Although it often appeared that Red Guard action was spontaneous, it was not only officially sanctioned but was also officially directed. Xie Fuzhi (Hsieh Fu-chi), the Minister for Public Security, in addressing the police forces revealed both why it was that the Red Guards had such a free hand in their terror campaign and how they were able to target their victims so easily:

1   I am not for beating people to death. But when the masses hate the bad
   elements so deeply that we are unable to stop them, then don't try. The
   police should stand on the side of the Red Guards and establish contact
   with them, develop bonds with them and provide them with informa-
5   tion about the people of the five categories, landlords, rich peasants,
   reactionaries, bad elements, and rightists.

The names and locations of those listed in the 'five categories' were passed on to the Red Guard detachments who then descended upon their victims. In 1996 Ze Rong recalled his behaviour as a thirteen-year-old Red Guard:

1   I was a leader of one of the city-wide Red Guard organisations and our
   job was to attack the homes of class enemies. We noticed the Red
   Guards in Beijing did it and instead of being punished were praised by

the Communist leaders. So, we followed their lead. We found out the
5 names and addresses of the Rightists, landlords and 'bad elements' and
drove to their homes in our school truck. When we found the heads of
each household, we read out quotations from Mao's little red book.

Then, we loaded all their valuables, especially gold, into the lorry and
10 carted them off for storage in the local Catholic Church. There were
mountains of stuff there: furniture, cases, pianos, and many Western
things that I had never seen before. Some of those whose homes we
ransacked were also beaten to death.

On a trip to the Babaoshan cemetery, I remember asking the man in
15 charge of the furnaces how many bodies had been burned as the Red
Guard terror got under way. It came to a figure of more than 2,000
people tortured to death in a period of just two weeks.

As had happened during the Stalinist purges in the USSR in the
1930s, so, too, in China's Cultural Revolution, the victimisers became
in turn the victims. Revolutionaries struggled to prove their proletarian integrity by becoming ever more extreme. Those who faltered
or showed signs of being sickened by the horrors were condemned as
reactionaries and found themselves subjected to the savagery that
they had recently meted out. Genuine idealism was swiftly corrupted
into unthinking brutishness. A young female student recorded:

1 One time on my way home I saw some Red Guards arresting a young
girl. They said she was a bad element. Whether she was or not was
beside the point. There was no investigation or legal process. Someone
said she was a baddie and that was enough. So they were using their
5 belts to beat her up. I was a Red Guard, too, and my first thought was
that I must express my revolutionary spirit. I took off my belt and lifted
it high as if I too was taking part in the beating. I couldn't actually bring
myself to hit her but I knew I had to look as if I was. Beating people was
a symbol of revolutionary fervour. If you didn't beat people you weren't
10 showing a proper hatred for the enemy or a proper love for the people.

The sheer zealotry of the Red Guards soon led the movement to turn
in on itself. Regional groups began to clash with one another. Factory
workers formed their own detachments and challenged the claim of
the student units to be the true leaders of the movement. The various
groups began to go to ever greater lengths to prove the purity of their
ideology and the depth of their loyalty to Mao. Most significant of all
was the role of the PLA. Initially the army had supported the students
and workers in hunting down class enemies but it was unwilling to
share its prestige as the creator and defender of China's revolution.
The PLA claimed a special relationship with Chairman Mao and with
the Chinese people, which entitled it to take over the Cultural
Revolution. Army units travelled throughout China in a campaign to
impress upon the people the intensity of PLA loyalty to Mao Zedong.

There is a strong case for suggesting that the anarchy associated with the Cultural Revolution was more apparent than real. The Red Guards were allowed to run wild only because Mao knew that at any time he could use the PLA to pull them back into line. In all its essentials the Cultural Revolution was directed from the top by Mao and his associates. It may often have had the air of spontaneity and it is true that once started it seemed to generate a dynamic of its own. But there were guiding hands behind the marches and the thuggery. The Maoists was prepared to let things run to extremes but always seemed able to call a halt when it suited them. The idealistic youngsters who appeared to lead the Cultural Revolution were in fact pawns in the power struggle within the CCP.

4 Mao's Attempt to Reshape Chinese Culture

It has been a characteristic of totalitarian regimes that they have tried to consolidate their hold not simply by modifying the culture they inherit but by totally changing it. Lenin, Stalin, Hitler and Mao each claimed in their different ways that what they intended was the establishment not merely of a new political order but of a new society.

The role of creator-in-chief of the new Chinese culture was taken by Mao's wife, Jiang Qing. It was she who became directly responsible for turning Mao's general denunciation of China's 'four olds' into a definite programme for the suppression of traditional Chinese society. Jiang applied a rigid system of censorship which denied a public showing or performance to any work which did not meet her criteria of revolutionary purity. Only those writings, art works, broadcast programmes and films which had directly relevant contemporary Chinese themes were permitted. This drastically reduced the number of acceptable works. The whole canon of Western classical music was banned. Traditional Chinese opera was ruled out and replaced by a repertoire of eight grindingly tedious contemporary works, concerned in the most naive fashion with the triumph of the workers over their class enemies. Taste and quality were sacrificed to the demand that culture must serve the people by having as its only theme the struggle of the heroic masses. Frances Wood, who was living in Beijing at the time of the Cultural Revolution recorded:

1   It doesn't matter whether you are talking about opera, theatre, novels or even poetry, people had to be either black or white. You couldn't take anything from the past and discover that it fitted in to these incredibly strict rules. I mean any work of art of any subtlety has got grey charac-
5   ters in it, so it was essential to sweep everything away. It's true also that, for example, a lot of things to do with the past are politically incorrect because history had to be reinterpreted, so you couldn't use something that talked about the Dowager Empress [the notorious Qing matriarch who died in 1908] in any terms other than absolute condemnation.
10 History had been re-written as cowboys and indians, so you had nothing

to lean on, you had to start again with this new pure drama and pure opera and pure fiction.

Underlying this sweeping form of thought control was Jiang's development of the Marxist-Leninist notion that culture is essentially an expression of the political and social circumstances in which it is created. No form of art can be neutral or detached. Nor can it possess an intrinsic value separate from its class origins. Every culture is a direct product of the society from which it springs. A feudal society can produce only a feudal culture, a bourgeois society only a bourgeois one. Therefore, in the socialist society of the PRC the feudal arts of imperial China and the bourgeois arts of the West had no place. They must be wholly eradicated and their place taken by the truly proletarian arts, representing the glorious struggle of the workers against class oppression. Jiang Qing's rejection of all non-proletarian culture was political correctness in its most extreme form. It was an intellectually and emotionally destructive process that aimed at the systematic undermining of all sense of tradition. The prevailing slogan was 'the more brutal, the more revolutionary'. Children were made to trample grass and knock the heads off flowers in order to show their resolve not to be seduced by decadent bourgeois concepts of beauty. It was laid down that to allow love or family affection to dictate one's behaviour was to give in to bourgeois sentimentality. A Beijing student recalled:

1   From the first day of my schooling, at seven years old, I learned 'I love you Chairman Mao', not 'I love you Mamma or Papa'. I was brainwashed for eight years and looking back I realise that the Party was doing everything to keep us pure, purifying us so we would live for Mao's idealism,
5   Mao's power, instead of discovering our own humanity.

Zhou Guanrun (Chou Kwan-run), a professor of music, recalled how Jiang's edicts against bourgeois culture terrorised the staff at the Beijing Conservatoire into silence.

1   No music sounded any more. The Conservatoire was silent. Everybody was just learning and doing self-criticism or accepting criticism from students. So we had to come every day, every morning at the time of office hours and sit there and read books and then do criticism. We had
5   to analyse our mistakes in our work, our teaching or performing, because we performed a lot of classical or Chinese traditional music. We thought that we popularised the bad things to the young generation.

By the early 1970s Jiang Qing's assault on traditional culture had begun to produce an artistic wasteland. Musicians, painters and writers who showed reluctance to conform to the new rigidities were denounced and sent to 're-educational' labour camps. Zhou Guanrun was one such victim:

1   We were working in the rice fields and we had to scrape our own
     fingers into the ground to loosen it. We thought perhaps it would be
     quite clever if we had some tools to do that but the soldiers said 'no
     way - you have to be educated to do everything with your fingers'. That
5   was very painful to us because for a pianist like me scraping all the time
     into the ground hurt my fingers. I just thought that I would never play
     again, because during the Cultural Revolution I thought I will never do
     music again, never play piano again.

Before his fall from grace Deng Xiaoping dared to suggest that
culture was about entertainment as well as indoctrination. He
remarked sardonically, 'After a hard week's work people want to go to
the theatre to relax and you go to the theatre and watch Jiang Qing's
pieces and you are on a battle field'. But with the exception of Deng
none of the leading politicians was prepared to challenge Jiang's
policy of cultural barbarism. They, like the majority of artists, opted
publicly to approve her great cultural experiment while privately
hoping that its excesses would soon be over once the rapidly ageing
Mao had died and Jiang's power had been broken. It is true that some
of the restrictions were lifted in the early 1970s. The visit of President
Nixon to China in 1972 coincided with some softening of the artistic
hardline. In 1973 the London Philharmonic Orchestra was invited to
Beijing where its performances were greeted with massive public
enthusiasm. But in the following year the Chinese were firmly told
that such re-opening of contacts with the West was not to be interpreted as a weakening of the Cultural Revolution. Chinese orchestras
were still forbidden to perform Western works. The *Peking Review* gave
its readers a sharp reminder of where their cultural loyalties lay:

1   Some people talk about bourgeois classical music with great relish, are
     mesmerized by it and prostrate themselves before it, showing their
     slavish mentality for all things foreign. They are nihilists with regard to
     national art. Their reverence for foreign things is actually reverence for
5   the bourgeoisie. If this erroneous thinking of extolling foreign things and
     belittling Chinese things is not criticized and repudiated, then prole-
     tarian art and literature will not be able to develop and Chairman Mao's
     revolutionary line in art and literature cannot be implemented.

Jiang's stranglehold on the arts remained for the whole of the decade
between 1966 and Mao's death ten years later. By then it was clear that
the result of this artistic persecution had not been the creation of a
new culture but merely the destruction of the old one. Writers and
artists had been frightened either into inaction or into producing
dross that would not fall foul of the censors. Yan Yen, a poet, reflected
on the profound damage done to China: 'As a result of the Cultural
Revolution you could say the cultural trademark of my generation is
that we have no culture.'

5 The Cultural Revolution - The Final Phase

By the late 1960s things appeared to be out of hand in the country at large. What amounted to civil war was raging in China. Rival Red Guard factions were in open conflict with each other and with the PLA. The widespread disruption, which had brought industrial production to a halt and closed the schools and universities, seemed to be pushing China towards economic and social collapse. Mao and his supporters decided that matters had gone far enough. Orders were given that the work of the Red Guards should be taken over by the PLA. This did not mean a weakening of the campaign against the anti-Maoists. Indeed, the PLA squads who replaced the Red Guards were, if anything, even more vicious in their persecution of 'counter-revolutionaries'.

The government decided to redirect the energy and idealism of the young people who had made up the Red Guard movement. Another great campaign was announced which called on the youngsters 'to go up to the mountains and down to the villages'. They were urged to go into the countryside and live among the peasants; in this way they would experience the dignity of labour and deepen their under-standing of revolution. But the real motive was to rid the urban areas of the gangs of delinquent youths who had threatened to become uncontrollable in the general turmoil. The campaign may also be seen as an extension of Mao's policy for making city intellectuals experience the harsh realities of life that were the common lot of the ordinary Chinese.

Yet whatever the ulterior motives underlying the campaign, there was no doubting that it did arouse a genuine response. Between 1967 and 1972 over twelve million young people moved from the towns into the countryside. The idealism of those who made up this great experiment rarely survived the grim conditions and appallingly low standards of living that they met; it is doubtful that more than a small minority felt they had gained from the experience.

As the 1970s wore on there were signs that many Chinese were becoming disenchanted with the Cultural Revolution. Despite this, there was little overt opposition to Mao. Mistakes were blamed on those responsible for implementing Mao's policies, never on Mao himself. The cult of Mao Zedong was by now so well established that while he lived there was no realistic possibility of undermining his authority. What happened, therefore, was that the power seekers in the CCP declared their unalloyed loyalty to the Great Helmsman and jockeyed for position and influence while awaiting his death which, judging from the rumours that leaked out about his declining health, could not be long delayed.

a) The Fall of Lin Biao

There was one major exception to the practice of wait and see. In an extraordinary set of events, Lin Biao, the nominated successor to Mao, became a victim of the Cultural Revolution that he had done so much to engineer. As is so often the case with internal Chinese politics, the exact details are difficult to determine. However, in outline what appears to have happened is that by 1971 Mao or those closest to him had become disturbed by the growing influence that Lin Biao and the PLA were acquiring under the Cultural Revolution. Lin and other PLA leaders were told, therefore, that they must submit themselves to self-criticism. Interpreting this as the first step in a strategy to remove him from power, Lin became a conspirator in a desperate plot to assassinate Mao. When the plot was discovered Lin attempted to escape to the USSR. On 13 September 1971 the jet plane carrying him and his family crashed in Inner Mongolia, killing all on board. Whether it was an accident or sabotage remains a mystery. Mao insisted that he had not ordered the shooting down of the plane. Nonetheless, his most dangerous rival had been removed.

The news of the scandal surrounding Lin's fall was not publicly released until a year later in 1972. When it was announced it was as the basis of a 'criticise Lin Biao and Confucius' campaign. The name of Lin Biao 'the great traitor and Soviet spy' was linked with the great reactionary figure of Chinese history. It was this public denunciation of Lin, a man who only a short while before had been second only to Mao in popular estimation, that led many to question privately whether they could any longer believe the official pronouncements issued by the PRC authorities. The sudden and baffling changes in the reputation of political leaders created the gravest doubts as to whether any government statement was trustworthy. A Chen villager later admitted:

1 When Liu Shaoqi was dragged down we'd been very supportive. At that
   time Mao Zedong was raised very high: he was the red sun and what
   not. But the Lin Biao affair provided us with a major lesson. We came to
   see that the leaders up there could say today that something is round;
5 tomorrow, that it's flat. We lost faith in the system.

b) The Re-Emergence of Zhou Enlai and Deng Xiaoping

One important consequence of Lin Biao's dramatic exit was the enhancement of Zhou Enlai's position in the government and party. Zhou was one of the great survivors of Chinese politics. His shrewd sense of political judgement and genuine popularity enabled him to evade the attempts made to isolate him during the Cultural Revolution. It was Zhou who had worked to prevent the fracturing of the Party during the power struggles of the 1960s and it was he who became recognised as an outstanding international statesman in the 1970s. Concerned to improve China's economy by increasing its world trade and inward investment, Zhou was the major negotiator in the talks that led to the re-establishing of commercial and cultural links with the West, symbolised by the visit of President Nixon to China in 1972. (See page 93.)

This lifting of the 'bamboo curtain' also benefited Deng Xiaoping, another great survivor in the maelstrom of PRC politics. His earlier dismissal for having been a 'capitalist roader', a reference to his wish to see the economy modernised, now worked to his advantage. In 1973 Zhou Enlai, who had great respect for Deng's detailed knowledge of the workings of the CCP, invited him to re-enter the government. By 1975 Deng had regained his place as Party Secretary. But his rehabilitation did not go unchallenged. Jiang Qing and the Maoists, disturbed by the grip that the moderates appeared to be regaining, turned the 'criticise Lin Biao and Confucius' campaign into an attack upon 'the pragmatist clique', a reference to Zhou and Deng.

The influence that Jiang and the Maoists still exercised was evident in the crisis that followed the death of Zhou Enlai in January 1976. With his moderating influence now removed, the power struggle took another turn. In April, the memorial service for Zhou, held in the Great Hall of the People facing Tiananmen Square, became the occasion for a large-scale demonstration in favour of the policies that he had advocated. A crowd numbering tens of thousands flocked into the Square to lay wreaths and pictures of Zhou around the Heroes Monument. This was a spontaneous gathering which defied the official order that there should be no public displays of mourning. Speeches were made that became increasingly bolder in tone, graduating from praise of Zhou Enlai for his wise statesmanship to attacks upon the government for its corruption. Fearing that the demonstration was becoming unmanageable, the Mayor of Beijing ordered riot police to remove the flowers and tributes and disperse the crowds. When some of the demonstrators resisted the police used force. Scattered but violent and bloody confrontations took place before the police managed to clear the Square.

The Politburo condemned this 'Tiananmen Incident' as the work of rightist agitators and laid a large part of the blame on Deng Xiaoping whom they dismissed from his position as Party Secretary. Although he had not been present at the demonstration, Deng chose not to risk defending himself; instead he removed himself from the political scene by hastily leaving Beijing for Guangdong province, there to wait on events.

c) The Death of Mao Zedong

No clear lead came from Mao Zedong for the simple reason that during the last year of his life he was rarely capable of giving one. His doctor, Li Zhisui, subsequently revealed that, during the last three years of his life, Mao was sustained only by massive injections of drugs which left him comatose for much of the time. The term 'helmsman' has a particular irony, for Mao now was quite unable to govern. It was this situation that gave such influence to his close attendants. They became the interpreters of his barely coherent utterances.

Yet even though Mao was incapacitated his power remained. In an odd way it was actually increased. Since he was so often enfeebled, it became increasingly difficult to know exactly what his ideas and instructions actually were. This had two conflicting consequences: it paralysed the fearful into inaction since they were frightened of taking steps that Mao might later condemn in one of his rational moments and it encouraged those who believed that Mao would never recover to try to manoeuvre themselves into a position from which they could subsequently seize power. This left Jiang Qing and the Gang of Four in effective control. However, their authority depended wholly on their closeness to Mao. Once he had died everything would be at hazard.

Given Mao's god-like status, it was somehow fitting that his death in September 1976 should have been preceded six weeks earlier by what many saw as an omen - a massive earthquake which wiped out the industrial city of Tangshan in Hebei province. This tragedy, one of the greatest natural disasters in Chinese history, claimed 800,000 casualties, a third of them fatalities. People recalled that in Chinese lore earthquakes, 'the speaking of the dragon', denoted the advent of great changes in the state. Mao had been deified in his own lifetime and when gods die the succession - as events were to show - becomes a troubled affair.

6 The Legacy of Mao's Cultural Revolution

The Cultural Revolution's purpose was nothing less than the creation of a new type of human being. As in the Soviet Union, where the ideologues who served Stalin had spoken of creating a new species, *homo sovieticus*, so in Mao's China the Cultural Revolution was an attempt to change human nature. But, in both countries, it proved far easier to destroy than to create. Few societies have undergone such an extraordinarily destructive phenomenon as the Cultural Revolution in China. Its economic consequences were disastrous. The turmoil in the schools and universities meant that education and training simply ceased. This created an industrial and agricultural torpor, the effects of which were to last for decades. Yet this was the least of the evils in this 'period of madness'. As one participant put it simply but tellingly, 'China lost its humanity'. The organised terror created a horrifying atmosphere of callousness and brutality.

The examples are legion. In Beijing itself, in addition to the daily scenes of beatings in the street, theatres and sports grounds became the venues of systematic killings of bound victims. During a two-day period in Daxing (Tsa-hsing) County, north of Beijing, 300 people were clubbed to death in the public square. In Guangxi (Kwangsi) province there were an estimated 67,000 deaths in the decade after 1966, while in Mongolia, Tibet and Sichuan the figures ran into hundreds of thousands. At the trial in 1980 of the Gang of Four, it was charged that the purges they had sanctioned had resulted in the killing of over half a million CCP officials. In the late 1970s, the social historian, Yan Jiaqi (Yan Chao-chi), calculated that the overall death figures for China amounted to several million.

Twenty years after the events, Deng Xiaoping's son, Pufang, reflected: 'The Cultural Revolution was not just a disaster for the Party, for the country, but for the whole people. We were all victims, people of several generations. One hundred million people were its victims'. Harry Wu, the noted Chinese dissident, who spent nineteen years as a political prisoner in the Laogai, China's equivalent of the USSR's Gulag, asserted that there were more than 1,000 labour camps in China, scattered across the country. He described them as:

1   The biggest concentration camp system in human history ... Everybody in China has suffered, or knows somebody who suffered. When the Red Guards were running around like madmen in the middle 1960s it was not really a case of us-against-them. It was us-against-us. Everybody
5   suffered.

But appalling though the physical brutality was, many Chinese now testify that it was the assault on the human spirit that was the most deadly. An atmosphere of violence prevailed throughout China. Language and thought was corrupted by it. In the words of a Chinese poet:

1   The Cultural Revolution abused rhetoric in a way that no one has ever done before or since. During the Cultural Revolution the propaganda run on the state media always described Chinese life in the most glowing language. It was only when I went to the countryside that I
5   suddenly discovered the conflict between language and reality and this gave me a profound distrust of the language of all this state propaganda.

Truth itself was a victim. The most extreme terms had been used to condemn those identified as opponents of the revolution. They were 'monsters', 'animals', 'freaks', who deserved no mercy. To be accused was to be guilty; ordered discussion and debate were impossible. Even now it is difficult for the Chinese to bring themselves to study the Cultural Revolution in detail. Most prefer to ignore altogether this period of collective madness. The memories are too painful. A representative voice of this sense of individual and collective shame is that of Lo Yiren, a poet's daughter, who had been a Red Guard in her youth: 'We became beasts. There was not a human being left in China.

We were worse than beasts. At least beasts do not slaughter their own kind.'

Much remains to be researched concerning the Cultural Revolution. Mao, of course, initiated it, but it needed countless others to carry it out. What were the motives of such people? Perhaps the enthusiasm and extremism with which the policy was implemented is explained by long-existing local rivalries and personal vendettas. It is known that Stalin's purges in the USSR could not have been carried out without the willingness of so many to engage in exploitation and terror. So much of the Cultural Revolution was organised hate. This began with Mao himself. Chen Hansheng who knew Mao personally defined him as 'a person of hatred'. Mao often spoke of the ruthlessness with which China's revolution had to be pursued. He drew parallels between his own position and that of the Emperor Qin Shi Huang (Shih Huang-ti) whose huge terra cotta army has been unearthed at Xian (Sian). It was Qin (221-210 BC) who presided over the enforced unification of the Han state, often regarded as the birth of China as a nation. The comparison was apt; Qin had traditionally been described as one of the bloodiest rulers in Chinese history. Li Rui, who had been a personal secretary to Mao in the early years of the PRC, defined the Cultural Revolution as 'Marx plus Emperor Qin'.

Other historical parallels help to explain the character of the Cultural Revolution. Manifest in the history of China after 1949 are the oppressive tendencies, discernible in all totalitarian regimes, that culminate in purges and blood letting. Deliberately-ordered mass destruction and extermination took place in Hitler's Germany, Stalin's Russia, and Pol Pot's Cambodia. But nothing has ever occurred on the scale of the Chinese experience. Taken together, the Great Leap Forward and the Cultural Revolution resulted in the deaths of over thirty million people. The scale was so staggering that for a long time neither Chinese nor Western scholars could bring themselves to accept it. What made the horror so difficult to contemplate, let alone understand, was that it had been perpetrated in the name of a philosophy that claimed to have found the scientific means to end human exploitation and misery.

Studying 'China Under Mao'

The chapters on Mao's China can be conveniently broken down into three main sections: 1. The consolidation of Communist power; 2. Mao's economic policies; 3. The Cultural Revolution. Each of these themes raises questions which are central to an examination of Mao's exercise of power in China.

1. **The consolidation of Communist power**
    Key Question: How effectively had the CCP established its authority over China by 1966?

Sections 1 and 2 of this chapter are the obvious required reading but added perspective will be gained by consulting Sections 1 to 3 of the Introduction and Section 1 of Chapter 2.

Points to Consider: 'Effectively' is the critical term. It is best approached by listing the problems confronting the CCP after its victory in 1949 and then assessing how closely the government came to resolving them. The problems can be broken down into a number of categories, such as military, economic and political. Under military difficulties reference might well be made to the presence on the mainland of remnants of the GMD who still represented a threat to the new regime, and the CCP's need to consolidate its hold over the outlying areas of China. The outstanding economic problems were acute food shortages and lack of industrial development, while the demanding political problem was that of establishing the governmental authority of the CCP in a country that had known only instability and impermanence during the preceding forty years. You could argue that the CCP's military achievements were wholly successful since by the end of the 1950s no part of China offered a serious challenge to the control of the PLA. On the economic front, a provocative line of thought you might examine is whether Mao used collectivisation and the five-year plans primarily as a means of solving agricultural and industrial problems or as a way of increasing the CCP's grip on the nation. The social upheaval and widespread famine were glaring economic failures, but were they intended to be part of the process by which the government extended its authority? You may wish to consider whether collectivisation belongs with the anti-campaigns, the creation of the one-party state, the Great Leap Forward and the Cultural Revolution as forms of political and social control that crushed all vestiges of opposition and left the CCP with absolute authority over China.

2. Mao's Economic Policies

Key Question: Consider the view that 'the PRC's economic policies under Mao were fundamentally flawed'.

Sections 3 and 4 of Chapter 2 are the most relevant reading but it would also be helpful to refer to Sections 1 to 3 of the Introduction.

Points to Consider: The key term to be defined is 'fundamentally flawed'. It invites you to distinguish between the conception and the execution of the policies. You might well note that Mao never acknowledged that his policies had failed. When eventually told of the scale of the famine which collectivisation had helped to create, his response was to blame it on administrative mistakes. As was said in relation to the previous question the line between Mao's economic and political strategies was often a thin one. The point is highly relevant here. In ideological terms it was essential that the peasants be brought under control. It would be worth discussing whether Mao was therefore less concerned with advancing China economically than with using economic means to establish authority over China. Some space in your answer should be given to examining the policies themselves. If you consider they were based on the false notion that collectivisation of itself would lead to greater food production and that mass labour rather than advanced technology would lead to industrial growth you have strong grounds for arguing that Mao's policies were indeed fundamentally flawed. On the other hand it would add balance to your answer if you were to stress the sheer scale of the economic problems that China faced in 1949 and to add that, whatever the shortcomings of the CCP's economic planning, the fact was that Communist China did survive.

3. The Cultural Revolution

Key Question: How far did China's Cultural Revolution fulfil the dictum that 'in order to create it is first necessary to destroy'?

All sections of Chapter 3 are relevant here; reference should also be made to Section 2c of Chapter 1.

Points to Consider: The quoted words take you straight to the heart of the problem as Mao saw it in his declining years. You should ask yourself what was he trying to create and what did he think needed to be destroyed. List the weakness that he perceived. These might include his notion that the CCP had become stultified by the 1960s and that the party and government had lost their revolutionary edge and so were in danger of destroying all that had been achieved since 1949. His wish to leave Maoism permanently entrenched in China deserves consideration, as does his concept of 'continuing revolution'. His apparent willingness to unleash anarchy in China in 1966 certainly seems to fit the idea of destroying in order to create. But the 'how far' part of the questions invites you to apply some subtlety. While it is easy to see what was being destroyed it is more difficult to see what was being created. You would be entitled to point out that the upheaval of the Cultural Revolution, far from creating a new China, was essentially a reactionary enterprise aimed at leaving Mao's CCP in still tighter control. Even Jiang Qing's attempts to destroy Chinese culture are best understood not as a cultural phenomenon but as a process for removing all traces of political opposition within Maoist China.

Source analysis - 'China Under Mao'

There is a recommended formula for analysing documentary sources that guards against omitting any essential points. Extracts are examined under three main headings: 1 - context, 2 - meaning, 3 - significance. 1 locates the piece, describing where and when it was written or appeared. 2 explains the meaning and, where appropriate, the purpose of the text. It is in this section that particularly important or difficult terms are defined. Heading 3 provides the opportunity to expand upon the meaning of the source and relate it to wider themes.

The source analysis in the study guides in this book follows this three line approach.

The following is an analysis of three related documents central to the theme of 'the Cultural Revolution'. These appear on pages 45, 46 and 49-50.

1 - Context

The first extract comes from an account by the resident British journalist, Anthony Grey, of the extraordinary atmosphere in Beijing in 1966 at the beginning of the Cultural Revolution. The second is drawn from the reminiscences of a thirteen-year-old Red Guard in 1966. The third comes the reflections of a professor of music in 1966 who became a victim of the Red Guards.

2 - Meaning

Anthony Grey describes the veneration in which Mao was held by the ordinary Chinese and likens it to the emperor worship that had existed in classical China. He also sees it as an illustration of the power of social conformity in China which Mao had chosen to exploit. Ze Rong recalls the extremism which the authorities encouraged among the young Red Guards; brutality became the norm. Under their Maoist slogans the youngsters launched terrifying attacks on the property and person of those accused of being 'bad elements'. The campaign against China's intellectuals is illustrated by Zhou Guanrun who describes how it became impossible to study and perform classical or Chinese traditional music. He then relates how in the camp where he had been sent for 're-education' the conditions were deliberately intended to break the spirit as well as the body.

3 - Significance

The value of the sources collectively is that they offer a set of highly graphic eye-witness accounts of the atmosphere and impact of the Cultural Revolution. Grey, who was soon to catch the world's headlines after being subjected to a particularly inhuman form of house arrest by the Chinese, provides an outsider's view. We learn from him that the love of the ordinary Chinese for Mao Zedong was originally a genuinely-felt if unthinking emotion. It belonged to the Chinese tradition of respect for authority. How effectively it was exploited is clear from the Ze Rong's recollections. The reactions of a thirteen year-old when told by authority that he could abandon all former restraints were explosive. The savage behaviour in which he engaged can be taken as typical of the whole Red Guard movement whose destructive impact was experienced in individual terms by Zhou Guanrun. The humiliation he suffered illustrates the anti-intellectual character of a movement dedicated to the destruction of traditional Chinese culture. The sources provide complementary insights into the great formative experience of modern China.

Summary Diagram
China Under Mao: The Cultural Revolution, 1966-76

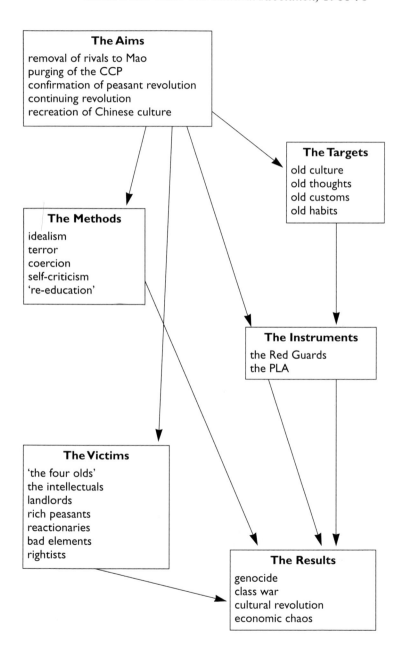

The Aims
removal of rivals to Mao
purging of the CCP
confirmation of peasant revolution
continuing revolution
recreation of Chinese culture

The Targets
old culture
old thoughts
old customs
old habits

The Methods
idealism
terror
coercion
self-criticism
're-education'

The Instruments
the Red Guards
the PLA

The Victims
'the four olds'
the intellectuals
landlords
rich peasants
reactionaries
bad elements
rightists

The Results
genocide
class war
cultural revolution
economic chaos

4 China After Mao: The Deng Era

Mao Zedong's hold over China had been so powerful that his death left a large political vacuum. How that vacuum should be filled has been the dominant issue in Chinese politics ever since.

The immediate problem for the Party after Mao's death was the practical one of what to do with his body. Should it be cremated, as Mao seemed to have wished, or should it be preserved for posterity in the way that Lenin's had been in the Soviet Union, embalmed and placed in a tomb that could then become a place of pilgrimage? Considerable debate went on before the latter choice was eventually agreed upon. Yet even then things went bizarrely wrong. The delay in reaching a decision meant that the corpse had begun to decompose. In the desperate attempt to make it presentable, at least until the funeral, a wild overestimate was made of the amount of preserving fluid that needed to be injected; more than four gallons of formaldehyde were pumped in. The corpse became so grossly swollen that it resembled a small barrage balloon. In the words of his doctor: 'Mao's face was bloated, as round as a ball, and his neck was now the width of his head ... His ears were swollen, too, sticking out from his head at right angles'. So, for twenty-four hours teams of attendants took turns to squeeze out the excess fluid through the skin and pummel the head and trunk back into something approaching a recognisable form. This macabre cosmetic exercise worked well enough to convince the grieving mourners who filed passed the body as it lay in state.

The problem of the disposal of Mao's mortal remains provides an apt metaphor for the deeper problem of what to do with Mao's political legacy. What that legacy was and who should succeed to it were the questions that now had to be answered.

1 The Power Struggle After Mao's Death

a) Hua Guofeng and the Gang of Four

At Mao's funeral, which was accompanied by displays of mass lamentation, there were indications that the jockeying for position among the Party leaders had already begun. Appearances matter greatly in Chinese politics. How prominent a role individuals played in the funeral ceremonies was a good indication of their place in the Party hierarchy. That Hua Guofeng delivered the main funeral eulogy was a clear sign of his precedence. He had stolen a march on Jiang Qing, whose unseemly behaviour at the lying in state, when she had fought with one of her cousins over the right to lay a wreath, had led the organisers of the ceremony to entrust her with only a minor role in the proceedings.

'With you in charge, my heart is at ease': these were the last intelligible words that Mao Zedong was reported to have uttered before he fell into a final coma. They were addressed to Hua Guofeng whom Mao, in the month before his death, had nominated as his successor as Party Chairman. Before his remarkable elevation Hua had been a little-known official with no substantial following in the Party. Insofar as Mao was capable of rational judgement in the last months of his life, his thinking appears to have been that with Zhou Enlai now dead, and Deng Xiaoping again demoted, there was no longer an obvious heir to the leadership of China. It was far better therefore to give authority to someone whose record, while undistinguished, had been one of unswerving Maoist loyalties.

It is particularly notable that Mao Zedong did not contemplate entrusting power to his wife, Jiang Qing, and her followers. This suggests that despite the ferocity with which the Gang of Four had tried to enforce their concept of Maoist orthodoxy upon China, Mao himself had always been suspicious of their motives. His personal estrangement from Jiang - they lived apart for at least the last ten years of Mao's life - may well have been deepened by their political differences. In the rigidity of their ideology the Gang of Four were more Maoist than Mao. It is worth noting that it was Mao himself who first coined the disparaging term, the 'Gang of Four', to describe Jiang Qing and her three closest associates, Zhang Chunquiao (Chang Chun-chiao), Yao Wenyuan (Yao Wen-yuan), and Wang Hongwen (Wang Hung-wen). All three men had risen to prominence in the Shanghai section of the CCP and had become members of the Politburo. Zhang was a ruthless political infighter who had clawed his way to the top in Shanghai. Yao was an aggressive ideologue, whose denunciation of Wu Han's play, *The Dismissal of Hai Rai from Office*, had precipitated a political storm in 1965 (see page 36). Wang Honwen had made his mark as a trade union leader in Shanghai and had earned a fearsome reputation for the viciousness with which he had led the Cultural Revolution in that city; thousands of deaths were attributed to him.

Immediately following Mao's passing the sixteen-member Politburo split into two identifiable groups - the Gang of Four, and the supporters of Hua Guofeng. Since the Gang were in a minority, they were bound to lose in any straight votes. But, although the Politburo was undoubtedly the dominant body politically, there was always the possibility that its power could be neutralised by a direct resort to military force. This was where Hua Guofeng's previous dealings with the army stood him in good stead. He was able to outflank the Gang of Four. His work as co-ordinator of the relief effort that had followed the Tangshan earthquake in 1976 had consolidated his close relationship with a number of generals. In particular, he had gained the support of Wang Dongxing (Wang Tung-hsing), head of the special security forces, and Marshall Ye Jianying (Yeh Chien-ying), chief of

Beijing's armed forces. Wang had earlier been an associate of the Gang of Four but had never fully committed himself to their side. This was largely because he found Jiang Qing's hectoring style deeply distasteful. A similar personal dislike of Jiang had also helped push Marshall Ye into direct opposition to the Gang of Four. It was also significant that Mao during the last year of his life had made Ye a close confidant, warning him of Jiang's overweening ambitions. On Mao's death. therefore, both Wang Dongxing and Marshall Ye were prepared to prevent the Gang of Four from seizing power.

As had invariably been the case in China in a disputed succession, it was the military who held the key. Had the Gang of Four been able to command enough army support they might well have been able to assert political control. Realising this, the Gang tried to exploit their provincial connections. They hoped to be able to use their influence in Shanghai, where they had their strongest following, to raise an army from the city's militia. They had some success but the troops available to them were never sufficient to match their political ambitions. The reality was that the Gang's provincial base was too detached from the real source of power in Communist China - Beijing. How little influence the Gang had in the capital was shown when Jiang Qing's main military supporter, Mao Yuanxin (Mao Yuan-hsin), a nephew of Mao Zedong, was dismissed from his Beijing post by Marshall Ye. Mao Yuanxin had been given responsibility for collecting his late uncle's papers; Jiang had tried to bribe him into either finding evidence among these that Mao Zedong had wanted the Gang of Four to succeed him or into providing reliable forgeries to the same effect. (This was to be one of the allegations against Jiang at her later trial.) But with Mao Yuanxin's removal this particular ruse was blocked.

Jiang's other main hope had been that Wang Hongwen from his government post in Zhonganhai (Beijing's equivalent to Whitehall) would be able to organise support for the Gang of Four from other parts of China. It was the fear that Wang's efforts were beginning to work that precipitated the next move by their opponents. Fearing an attempted coup by the Gang, Marshall Ye and Wang Dongxing joined Hua Guofeng in a pre-emptive strike. Ye and Wang deployed selected units of the armed forces in Beijing and other key areas to forestall possible 'counter revolution'. Hua, in apparent innocence, then asked the Gang of Four to attend a rearranged Politburo meeting on 6 October. Each of the four was given a different time for the start of the meeting. When the three male members of the Gang arrived at their separate times they were immediately arrested. Before she had time to leave for the meeting, Jiang Qing was seized in her own home and bundled off to prison shouting obscenities at her captors. For a brief period it seemed that the Gang's supporters in Shanghai might actively challenge the turn of events in Beijing, but by the time the news of the Gang's fall was officially announced nationwide on 15 October all signs of resistance had disappeared.

b) the Re-Emergence of Deng Xiaoping

The ousting of the Gang of Four seemed to indicate that Hua Guofeng had inherited Mao Zedong's authority. But appearances were deceptive. The real beneficiary of the political manoeuvres that followed Mao's death proved to be someone who had played no direct part in them - Deng Xiaoping. Despite his withdrawal to Guangzhou following his earlier demotion, Deng retained the highest reputation and the largest following in the Party and in the PLA. This allowed him to play a waiting game during the power struggle. He did not need to challenge Hua Guofeng openly; he could rely on Hua's lack of genuine popularity in the Party denying him full power. This proved a shrewd calculation. Notwithstanding the enthusiasm which greeted his staged public appearances, Hua found his newly-acquired status within the party hard to sustain. There was a broad feeling among members that his position as Chairman was merely that of a caretaker. Hua was often ridiculed behind his back. Party members mocked his attempt to emphasise his physical resemblance to the Great Helmsman by brushing back his hair, puffing out his moon cheeks, and adopting Mao's plain blue-suited style of dress. They were quick to jeer at what they termed his two 'whatevers', a reference to Hua's often repeated summary of his approach to government: 'Whatever Mao said was right, whatever Mao did must be continued'.

The diminutive Deng Xiaoping could not hope to match Hua in the matter of physical characteristics, but he had no need of such tricks. Deng's strength lay in his reputation and his range of contacts within the Party and the PLA. Although Deng had been demoted during the Cultural Revolution, he had never lost his party membership. Now that Mao had gone and the Gang of Four had been removed there was no one who could match Deng Xiaoping's personal standing.

Deng was a natural survivor; he had an instinctive feel for politics, which showed itself in his ability to read situations and in his judgement of the right people to cultivate. One such was General Xu Shiyou (Hsu Shih-yu), the military governor of Guangzhou. Following his strategic withdrawal from Beijing, Deng had put himself under the protection of Xu, a determined opponent of the Gang of Four and no supporter of Hua Guofeng. Xu's influence was strong throughout the southern and eastern provinces, which were the most prosperous and economically advanced areas of China. He used his contacts with the leading CCP officials in these regions to press for Deng's reinstatement in the Politburo. Since Deng's earlier dismissal could be blamed on the intrigues of the now disgraced Gang of Four this proved relatively easy to achieve.

The most significant figure at this juncture was Marshall Ye Jianying. His support for Hua Guofeng had been provisional. He had backed him in order to overthrow the Gang of Four; that accomplished, his allegiance passed from Hua to Deng Xiaoping. In the Politburo, Ye became the chief spokesman for all those regional party leaders who demanded that Deng's value to the Party and the nation should be recognised by his re-admittance. Deng bided his time, not returning to Beijing until he was convinced that the Politburo's invitation to him to rejoin provided a genuine opportunity to regain power at the centre of things.

For the next two years Deng's influence in the party continued to grow at the expense of Hua's. Hua did not step down immediately. He retained his position as premier until 1980, but his political strength was leaking away. The majority of new members elected to provincial and national party committees were Deng's supporters. Hua attempted to fight a rearguard action by appealing for support to the PLA, but Deng's popularity with the army was too strong to be seriously undermined. What added to Deng's strength was his reputation on the economic front. It was Deng who had worked with Zhou Enlai in the 1970s in drafting 'the four modernisations', a major programme for the growth of the Chinese economy.

Developments in foreign affairs further accentuated the shift of power to Deng. He was widely seen as the natural successor to China's greatest international statesman, Zhou Enlai. While Mao Zedong had formally represented China in world affairs, it had been Zhou who had been the PRC's chief spokesman and negotiator in all the major issues in foreign policy between 1949 and 1976. Deng had often been his lieutenant. Deng's experience and reputation in foreign affairs far outstripped that of Hua Guofeng. This was re-emphasised in 1978 and 1979 by Deng's personal leadership of separate Chinese delegations to Burma, North Korea, Japan, Thailand, Malaysia, and the USA (see page 93).

2 The Third Plenum, 1978 - The PRC's Turning Point

The Third Plenum of the 11th Central Committee of the CCP, which gathered in December 1978, proved to be a landmark in China's post-Mao reformation. Its resolution 'to restore Party democracy' began the process of rehabilitating those who had been wrongly condemned during the Maoist purges of the 1960s and 70s. This marked the final abandonment of the Cultural Revolution. The Plenum confirmed Deng's leadership of China by appointing him as Chairman of the People's Political Consultative Conference, the body that was to be foremost in initiating reform in China. In foreign affairs, it was the Third Plenum that first defined 'the one country, two systems' solution to the Taiwan and Hong Kong questions (see page 102). Its resolution on economic planning was in essentials an acceptance of Deng's 'four modernisations' programme.

1 The rapid development of the national economy as a whole and the steady improvement in the living standards of the people of the whole country depend on the vigorous restoration and speeding up of farm production, on resolutely and fully implementing the policy of
5 simultaneous development of farming, forestry, animal husbandry, side-occupations and fisheries, the policy of taking grain as the key link and ensuring an all-round development, the policy of adaptation to local conditions and appropriate concentration of certain crops in certain areas, and gradual modernisation of farm work.
10   Carrying out the Four Modernizations requires great growth in the productive forces, which in turn requires diverse changes in those aspects of the relations of production and the superstructure not in harmony with the growth of the productive forces, and requires changes in all methods of management, actions and thinking which
15 stand in the way of such growth. Socialist modernization is therefore a profound and extensive revolution.

The Third Plenum was a remarkable personal triumph for Deng Xiaoping. It put into practice what he had been urging since being invited back onto the Politburo. It also provided him with important political gains. 'Rehabilitation' meant the return to politics of two of Deng's strongest supporters, Peng Zhen (Peng Chen) and Bo Yibo (Po Yipo). The Plenum also chose to redefine the Tiananmen 'incident' of 1976, the occasion when public mourning for Zhou Enlai had turned into a large-scale anti-government protest (see page 53), as 'a genuinely revolutionary movement'. This meant that Deng, who had originally been blamed for encouraging the demonstration, was fully absolved from the charge of being a 'counter revolutionary', the accusation that had led to his demotion during the infighting that had occurred in the months before Mao's death.

Deng Xiaoping's successes at the Third Plenum showed that he had superseded Hua Guofeng in political authority. This was formalised in September 1980 when Hua resigned as premier, to be replaced by Deng's associate Hu Yaobang (Hu Yao-pang). Deng had himself been offered the position but had declined it on grounds of age. This was simple manoeuvring on his part; he had no intention of withdrawing from the scene and he knew, in any case, that formal designations and titles often belied the true disposition of power. Deng's honorary title was now 'paramount leader'. This had no specific functions attaching to it but was all the more powerful because of that. He feigned humility by declining to accept formal positions while knowing that he had the influence and connections to remain in control of developments. He was now in a position to begin what has become known as the Deng Revolution.

3 The Deng Revolution, 1979-89

a) The Legacy of Mao Zedong

Deng was anxious to rid China of the remnants of Maoism that stood in the path of progress, but he knew that Mao's impact had been so powerful that it could not be denounced without risking trauma and disruption in China. Deng judged that the Chinese people would not be able to comprehend an attack upon the 'Great Helmsman', the man who had created modern China and who had come to be regarded as a god. In the USSR, Stalin's record and reputation had become reviled within three years of his death in 1953. But there was to be no equivalent to de-Stalinisation in China. Any criticisms of Mao would have to be muted and subtle. Deng was well aware that an attack upon Mao would by implication be an attack on those who had served him. This would include all the current leaders of the government and the Party. Far safer, therefore, to subject Mao's reputation to the drip effect; let his reputation gradually erode rather than suffer a formal and official onslaught. A CCP Central Committee resolution of 1981, drafted by Deng Xiaoping himself, revealed the compromise the Party was obliged to make. It recorded that Mao Zedong had indeed been a great leader in his day, but one who had made errors which China was now entitled to correct: 'It is true that he made gross mistakes during the Cultural Revolution, but, if we judge his activities as a whole, his contribution to the Chinese Revolution far outweighs his mistakes'.

This key resolution came after another event which provided Deng and the reformers with a convenient opportunity to condemn Maoist ways while still appearing to honour Mao himself. In November 1980, over four years after their arrest, the Gang of Four were at last put on trial. The aim was to use them as scapegoats to explain why China had gone wrong. The general accusation was that they had betrayed Mao and the Chinese Revolution. Among the specific charges against them were that during the course of the Cultural Revolution they had been individually and collectively responsible for the deaths of 35,000 people and that they had 'framed and persecuted' a further three-quarters of a million. On trial with the Gang were Chen Boda (Chen Po-ta), Mao's former secretary and one of the hard-liners in the Cultural Revolution, and four senior officers, who were accused of having been implicated in Lin Biao's plot to assassinate Mao Zedong in 1971.

The delay in bringing the defendants to trial was explained by the new regime's expectation that a long period of captivity would break their spirit. The hope was only partly realised. Some of the accused appeared resigned to their fate. But Zhang Chunqiao's stubborn silence betokened contempt rather than acceptance of the court's proceedings. As for Jiang Qing, the principal figure, she remained totally defiant, refusing to accept the charges against her and shouting abuse at her accusers. The prosecution found it easy to characterise her frequent outbursts as evidence of her malice, perhaps even of her madness, but it was much harder to refute her insistent claim that Mao Zedong had backed her in all that she had done and that the Cultural Revolution had been carried out in accordance with his wishes. At one point she cried out: 'I was Mao's dog. Whoever he told me to bite, I bit'. The embarrassment caused throughout the three-month trial by Jiang's constant repetition of this point bore out the view of a number of the senior members of the CCP that the Gang of Four should not have been put on trial until they were all prepared to admit their guilt unreservedly. Political show trials are not about determining innocence or guilt according to the rules of evidence; they are an occasion for the authorities to assert control and to define orthodoxy.

The trials ended in January 1981 with guilty verdicts on all those charged. Jiang Qing and Zhang Chunquiao were sentenced to death, Wang Hongwen was imprisoned for life and Yao Wenyuan received a term of eighteen years. The remaining six defendants were given long prison sentences. The two death penalties were subsequently commuted to life imprisonment in order to give the convicted 'time to repent'. But Jiang Qing was not the repenting kind; at the time of

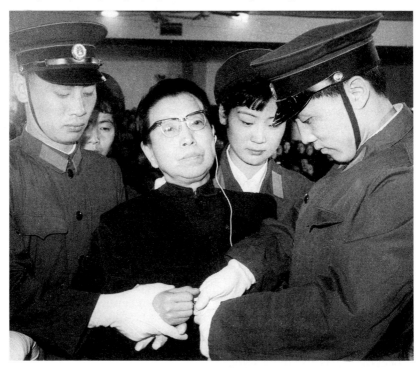

Jiang Qing at her trial in 1980

her death ten years later in 1991 (officially recorded as suicide although she had been suffering from throat cancer for some time), she was still angrily proclaiming her innocence.

The trials had been meant as a public purging of China's recent mistakes and to suggest that Deng's China had turned its back on the excesses of the Cultural Revolution. But while it was true that most Chinese believed that the Gang's vicious behaviour during that period certainly merited retribution, the conduct of the trial with its bullying tactics and attempts to humiliate the prisoners was not a good advertisement for Chinese justice. Foreign observers, who were either present in court or watched the proceedings on Chinese television, depicted the affair as one more in the series of show trials which had revealed the essentially totalitarian character of communist regimes from Stalin's onwards. Deng's push for party democracy and economic modernisation was clearly not to be interpreted as anything approaching liberalism in a Western sense.

b) Economic Reform

Throughout the 1970s, Deng in close alliance with Zhou Enlai, had advocated a departure from economic dogmatism. He had urged that in matters of industrial and agricultural planning a sense of realism ought to prevail. If a plan worked, keep it; if it did not, scrap it. If the market produced better results than rigid adherence to collectivist principles, then let the market operate freely. If contact with the capitalist West increased China's trade and commerce, then encourage such contact. This essentially pragmatic approach was summed up in Deng's favourite aphorism; 'It does not matter whether a cat is black or white, so long as it catches mice'.

During Mao's time, such apparent disregard for strict socialist planning had been unacceptable and was one of the reasons why Deng had become politically suspect. But with Mao dead and the Gang of Four, who had fiercely opposed the liberalising of the economy, defeated, the time to apply Deng's ideas had come. In 1982 Deng defined China's economic aims:

1 Invigorating our domestic economy and opening to the outside world are our long-term, not short-term, policies that will remain unchanged for at least 50 or 70 years. Our modernization programme is a socialist programme, not anything else. All our policies for carrying out reform,
5 opening to the outside world and invigorating the domestic economy are designed to develop the socialist economy. We allow the development of individual economy, of joint ventures with both Chinese and foreign investment and of enterprises wholly owned by foreign businessmen, but socialist public ownership will always remain predominant.
10 The aim of socialism is to make all people prosperous, not to create polarization.

It was to be an essentially 'hands off' policy. The state would not entirely detach itself from economic planning. The state owned enterprises (SOE) would remain the basic form of industrial organisation, but much greater freedom and initiative would be granted to managers and experts on the spot. Theory would give place to practicality. Purely administrative concerns would not be allowed to overrule economic considerations. Bureaucracy would be the servant not the master of the Chinese economy.

The 'four modernisations' programme, which aimed at the reform of agriculture, industry, defence, and education, did not initially represent a schematic and detailed plan. It was a set of objectives rather than a structured model. The objectives were clear but the means would be flexible. Successes would be built upon, failures would be jettisoned. Deng's reforms involved two main changes: the restoration of the market as the chief mechanism by which the economy operated and the opening of China to foreign trade. Mao's belief that China could be economically self-sufficient had proved a basic misjudgement; genuine growth required commercial expansion, domestic and foreign.

The reforms divide into two key sections and periods. Between 1978 and 1984, the main emphasis was on the improvement of the rural economy. After 1984, attention shifted to the development of industry and commerce.

c) Agriculture

In the countryside, the commune was abandoned and replaced by the 'xiang', a restoration of the original village or township. The xiang would still be required to meet government-determined output quotas, but, instead of these being achieved by the former collectivised work units or 'brigades', individual peasants and their families would now contribute their due share under a new 'household responsibility system'. Provided the peasants paid their taxes and contributed to the local quotas, they were to be left free to sell for private profit. As the following figures show, this policy of privatisation had notable success in the early 1980s:

The Effect of Privatisation on the Rural Economy			
	1957-78	1978-84	1984-88
Annual growth in grain production	2.0%	5.0%	-1%
Annual growth in agricultural value	1.4%	7.3%	3%

However, these figures also show that a relative decline set in after 1984. Grain output and agricultural values fell. The basic reason was that while the government had raised the prices being paid to the farmers for their produce it had not passed this increase on to the food buyers in the urban areas. This subsidising of both the producer and the consumer resulted in a national budget deficit. Matters had been made worse by the understandable decision of the farmers to switch their production from those crops that were subsidised least, such as grain, to those, such as rice, that received the largest procurement payment from the government. The result was a distortion of the normal rules of supply and demand which brought confusion and underproduction of essential foodstuffs.

Moreover, the benefits that privatisation and government subsidies brought the peasants were offset by the continuing uncertainty relating to property rights. Even with the land reforms introduced in the post-Mao era, the great majority of tenant farmers in China held their farms on a fifteen-year lease. In most cases privatisation had not granted permanent ownership; the legal position was that after fifteen years the land would revert back to the state. It is true that the government promised to consider extending the leases, but the bitter experiences of the Chinese peasants in the twentieth century had taught them to distrust government promises. Doubts about the security of their land holding deterred the peasants from improving their farms or investing for long-term growth. Hence the traditional but inefficient methods continued to prevail at the very time when the government believed its incentive schemes would lead the farmer to embrace modernisation and expansion.

d) Industry and Commerce

The relative success that had been achieved in agriculture by the mid-1980s enabled Deng and the government to turn their attention to industry. In pursuit of the two interlocking modernisations of industrial growth and scientific education, the universities were greatly expanded in size and number; the plan was to train one million technical students to become the managers and administrators of the new economy. The same objective underlay the schemes for sending thousands of Chinese students to study abroad; this was the means by which China would gain direct knowledge of Western technology and industrial methods. The fruits of this training and experience could then be applied in the Special Economic Zones (SEZ), regions which were earmarked for immediate and concentrated development. The first four SEZs were Shantou (Swatow) and Xiamen (Amoy) in the north, and Shenzen (Shentsen) and Zhuhai (Chuhai) in the south. These were the areas containing China's main export industries and foreign-owned companies. The SEZs became China's chief commercial outlets, modelled, although this was not officially acknowledged, on the Hong Kong pattern (see page 100). They were given regional autonomy and granted special tax concessions and financial freedoms to enable them to fulfil Deng's plea that the nation open up its commerce to the world. They proved to be one of modern China's success stories. Between 1981 and 1991, largely as a result of the developments in the SEZ, Chinese exports grew by over 500 per cent and inward foreign investment quadrupled. By the early 1990s China's trade was in balance and foreign investment in China had markedly increased.

Deng's pragmatism in economic matters was evident in all this. He had observed that where the younger and more progressive party officials had been allowed to put their ideas into practice the results had been striking. Two particular provinces, Sichuan and Guandong, had achieved major increases in productivity and output. Deng was impressed by the way the young managers in these regions had declined to be hidebound by the anti-capitalist dogmas of traditional Maoism and instead had adjusted their planning to the realities of supply and demand. They had achieved greater output and improved quality of product by introducing wage incentives to encourage the workers to develop efficient work practices and attain higher skill levels.

It was in regard to incentives that a major problem arose for Deng's reformers. In Mao's time, the State Owned Enterprises had been subject to total state control; prices, output targets and wages had all be fixed by the state. This had left little room for initiative. If an SOE proved cost effective it received no reward since any surplus it earned went straight to the state. Similarly, no matter how hard a worker toiled his wage rates did not vary. Whether he was conscientious or idle he still received the same income. Shielded from market forces by state protection, the SOEs and the workers in them enjoyed guaranteed employment and payment. In performance terms, this was stultifying since it destroyed any sense of endeavour. However, for the worker it provided an 'iron rice bowl', the Chinese term for a secure job for life. Moreover, the SOEs had also provided the workers with accommodation and medical and education benefits for their families. All these customary advantages now seemed to be jeopardised by the introduction of market forces into Chinese industry. Freedom from state control also meant the end of state subsidies. The SOEs were now expected to become efficient and competitive. Cost saving schemes were to be introduced as a means of achieving higher and cheaper output. New short-term contracts based on real labour-market needs meant that the employee would now be paid according to performance and would retain his job only if he contributed genuinely to the enterprise.

Not surprisingly, the industrial modernisation schemes met massive resistance from the SOEs. No matter how much the reformers emphasised the virtues of the new proposals, the workers were unwilling to put their 'iron rice bowl' at risk. This conservatism delayed the implementation of the reforms. It was not until 1986 that a modified labour-contract scheme could be introduced and even then it applied only to new employees not to established workers. The government offered further concessions in the form of unemployment insurance, but six years later the scheme covered barely one fifth of the eighty million employees in the SOEs.

Such reluctance to adopt new ways, together with China's great size and wide regional variations, would always make centrally-organised reform difficult to achieve. However, while these factors may have slowed down the rate of industrial growth they did not prevent major advances being made. The scale of China's economic progress under Deng is clear from the following figures:

China's Industrial Performance, 1979-94			
Year	Gross Domestic Product (in millions of yuan)	GDP Growth Rate (% pa)	Inflation Rate (% pa)	Manufacturing Output Growth Rate (% pa)
1979	732.6	7.6	6.1	8.6
1980	790.5	7.9	-1.5	11.9
1981	826.1	4.5	7.0	1.6
1982	896.3	8.5	11.5	5.5
1983	987.7	10.2	8.3	9.2
1984	1130.9	14.5	12.9	14.5
1985	1276.8	12.9	1.8	18.1
1986	1385.4	8.5	3.3	8.3
1987	1539.1	11.1	4.7	12.7
1988	1713.1	11.3	2.5	15.8
1989	1786.7	4.3	3.1	4.9
1990	1856.4	3.9	7.3	2.0
1991	2004.9	8.0	2.4	13.2
1992	2277.6	13.6	4.7	21.0
1993	2582.8	13.4	4.7	18.0
1994	2935.1	11.8	4.0	17.2

4 The Pro-Democracy Movement, 1979-89

a) Deng Xiaoping's Opposition to Political Reform

A point that is often missed by Western observers is that Deng's modernisation programme was as much concerned with political conservatism as it was with economic progress. He had emphasised this strongly when introducing his reforms. Deng balanced the Four Modernisations with what he called 'the Four Cardinal Principles', defined as 'keeping to the socialist road, upholding the people's democratic dictatorship, upholding leadership by the Communist

Party and upholding Marxism-Leninism and Mao Zedong Thought'. What is noticeable about these principles is that, unlike the Four Modernisations, they were not a formula for change but for the maintenance of the existing political structure. They were essentially a restating of the principle that the Chinese Communist Party had an absolute right to govern. It was only by the rule of the Party that China could be protected from corrupting Western political ideas and its true socialism preserved.

1   We are striving for socialist modernization, rather than other modern-
    izations. To preach bourgeois liberalization will lead our country to the
    capitalist road. We should take a clear-cut stand to uphold the Four
    Cardinal Principles and carry out a protracted struggle against bour-
    geois liberalization.

As Deng saw it, China's first need was for internal stability; without this the nation could not modernise and take its proper place in the world. Advocates of democracy were indulging in political luxuries that China could not afford:

1   Our goal is to create a stable political environment; otherwise we can
    accomplish nothing. Our task is to build up the country, and less impor-
    tant things should be subordinated to it. Even if there is a good reason
    for having them the major task must take precedence.
5   In 1980 the National People's Congress adopted a special resolution
    to delete from Article 45 of the Constitution the provision that citizens
    'have the right to speak out freely, air their views fully, hold great debates
    and write big-character posters'. Those who worship Western 'democ-
    racy' are always insisting on these rights. But having gone through the
10 bitter experience of the ten-year 'cultural revolution', China cannot
    restore them.
       Building socialism is our goal, but the way of approaching it must be
    determined by the particular conditions of our country. We propose to
    build socialism with Chinese characteristics.

Deng's aim was to restore the morale and standing of the CCP after the disruptive decades of the Great Leap forward and the Cultural Revolution. He wanted to show that the Communist Party was still capable of governing China and had the right to the loyalty of the people. It is broadly correct to see Deng Xiaoping as a reformer but only in the economic sphere. In politics he was a CCP hardliner. Like Mao Zedong, he was part product, part creator, of the turbulent history of China through which he had lived since the 1920s. His belief in the authority of the CCP as the only legitimate shaper of China's destinies was unshakeable. It was this conviction that made a major showdown between the old-guard CCP and the supporters of democracy increasingly likely.

b) The Growth of Protest

In the Avenue of Eternal Peace, near Tiananmen Square, there used to stretch a 200 metre brick wall. In the late 1970s the Avenue became a gathering place for students, who began to cover the wall with a mass of writings, ranging in size from small hand-written leaflets to large painted posters. The wall thus provided an obvious opportunity for the public expression of anti-government and anti-party feelings. Periodically, the government forbade the 'democracy wall' to be used in this way; it ordered the writings to be torn down and had the more outspoken of the critics arrested. One such occasion occurred early in 1979 when Wei Jingsheng (Wei Ching-chen), a former Red Guard, used the wall as part of his personal campaign to call the government to account for its failure to introduce real democratic freedoms into China. He was particularly critical of the PRC's recent foreign policy blunders. When Wei sought to reveal details of China's disastrous showing in Vietnam (see page 127), which the government had presented to the people as a great military success, he was arrested and later sentenced to fifteen years imprisonment.

Wei may be regarded as the first martyr in what became known as 'the democracy movement'. This was never an organised party and its composition and strength fluctuated, but it broadly represented those intellectuals who took hope from the abandonment of Maoism and interpreted Deng's reforms as offering the opportunity not only to modernise the economy but to liberalise the political system.The democracy movement did not initially challenge the legitimacy of the CCP; it appealed to Deng and the leaders of China to honour the principles that they professed. In particular, it asked that the Party's commitment to the rule of the people should not be a mere slogan but should be genuinely fulfilled by extending civil liberties, including voting rights, to the population at large. This was expressed in the demand that to Deng Xiaoping's 'Four Fundamentals' should be added a fifth - the adoption of democracy. For long periods the democrats were broadly tolerated but they were always likely to be turned on whenever the government felt objections had gone too far. This explains the severity of Wei's punishment. It was intended as a salutary warning to those intellectuals and journalists who mistakenly believed that the new democracy officially encouraged after Mao's death included the right to criticise the Party and government.

The criticism which most offended the authorities was that government in China had become corrupt. In the late 1970s a notorious case of racketeering came to light in Heilongjiang (Heilunkiang) province when it was revealed that the managers of a state-owned fuel and power company had been diverting large sums of public money into their own pockets. The chief embezzlers were put on public trial and executed. The government expected to gain credit from this widely-publicised example of its resolute response. But the fact was that the scandal had come to light only through the tenacity of an investigative journalist whose exposé forced the authorities to take action. Furthermore, the chief culprits in the Heilongjiang case were all leading members of the provincial CCP. Critics began to ask just how widespread was corruption within the Party.

The belief that there was something implicitly corrupt about the CCP's managment of China underlay the series of student demonstrations that occurred sporadically throughout the 1980s. The common demand of these protests was for greater political democracy and economic opportunity. Major disturbances occurred in 1986 in universities in Hefei (Hofei), Wuhan and Shanghai. Thousands of students followed Fang Lizhi (Fang Li-chih), a CCP member and a professor at Hefei, in calling for the open government and democracy that the authorities continually talked of but never delivered. The government quelled the disturbances by dismissing Fang, arresting the ringleaders, and characterising the troubles as the work of an anti-social minority. But how deeply the government had been shaken could be inferred from the dismissal of Hu Yaobang, the CCP General Secretary, and his replacement by Zhao Ziyang (Chao Tzuyang). It was charged that Hu had encouraged the student troubles by appearing to criticise the slow pace of political change. Deng thought it appropriate at this point to reiterate his condemnation of 'bourgeois liberalisation'. He defined this as the mistaken notion among some party members that modernisation involved moving towards Western-style democracy. After the crushing of the 1986 protests Deng spelled out why there could be no genuine democracy in China:

1   Since the defeat of the Gang of Four an ideological trend has appeared that we call bourgeois liberalization. Its exponents worship the 'democracy' and 'freedom' of the Western capitalist countries and reject socialism. This cannot be allowed. China must modernize; it must
5   absolutely not liberalize or take the capitalist road ...
      Democracy is an important means of carrying out our reform. But the question is how to put it into practice. Take general elections for instance. We run general elections at the lower levels, that is for country and district posts, and indirect elections at the provincial and municipal
10 levels. China is such a huge country, with such an enormous population, so many nationalities and such varied conditions that it is not yet possible to hold direct elections at higher levels. Furthermore, the people's educational level is too low. So we have to stick to the system of people's congresses, in which democratic centralism is applied ... Our
15 reform cannot depart from socialism, it cannot be accomplished without the leadership of the Communist Party. Socialism and Party leadership are inter-related; they cannot be separated. Without the leadership of the Communist Party, there can be no building of socialism.

Deng's statement captured the essential difference of outlook between the CCP conservatives and the pro-democracy movement and goes far towards explaining the disastrous events that were to occur in Beijing in 1989.

5 The Road to Tiananmen Square

In Beijing in the summer of 1989 an event took place which captured the attention of the world - the shooting in Tiananmen Square of thousands of unarmed demonstrators by detachments of the PLA. The massacre, carried out on government orders, had a significance far beyond its immediate occasion. It provided a commentary on all that had happened in China since Mao's death and exposed the underlying political problems that contemporary China has yet to solve. Before describing the tragedy and assessing its significance it is necessary to trace and explain the sequence of events that led up to it.

With hindsight, the massacre in June 1989 can be seen as the tragic climax to a decade of frustration. For many Chinese the period of Deng's reforms, 1979-89, proved deeply disappointing. After the initial economic spurt of the early 1980s there had been a serious downturn in agricultural and industrial production. Galloping inflation, the problem that had fatally weakened the Nationalists before 1949, destroyed the government's subsidy policy which had shielded the urban dwellers from high prices. China's ever-increasing population and the continuing movement of people from the countryside into the urban areas intensified the pressure on living space in the major cities and undermined the recently improved standards of living. It seemed that aspirations had been raised only to be dashed.

Economic disappointment became mixed with political grievance in the democracy movement. Students and intellectuals felt that, despite the promise of progress and reform held out by the modernisation programme, the party under Deng Xiaoping had failed to deliver. Poor job prospects were a particular anxiety among the students. In the late 1970s, in accordance with the four modernisations programme, there had been an explosion in the numbers entering higher education. But a decade later it was evident that employment opportunities had failed to keep pace with the rising number of graduates. There was anger that such jobs as were available were reserved for party members and their children. It was this grievance that fuelled the anger over government corruption.

In its early stages there was a striking similarity between the Tiananmen massacre of June 1989 and the Tiananmen incident of April 1976 (see page 53). Both were precipitated by the death of a leader who had been revered by the students as representing the progressive impulse in Chinese politics. On 15 April 1989, the death of Hu Yaobang focused the minds of all those who were unhappy with the economic and political system as it was operating under Deng Xiaoping. Hu had not always been sympathetic to the demands for greater democracy, but all that was forgotten at his passing. What was remembered was his removal from government in 1987 for daring to support the student protests. He had been forced to undergo self-criticism and had been subjected to such harsh treatment that his health had broken. Posthumously he was elevated by the students into a symbol of resistance whose death from a heart attack was blamed on the harassment he had suffered for having upheld democratic values. By the time of Hu's memorial service, which took place a week after his death, large crowds had gathered in the Square. They demonstrated noisily as three kneeling students tried to press a petition into the hands of Premier Li Peng and other government officials as they made their way into the Great Hall of the People to attend the service. The refusal of Li and his colleagues to accept the petition was taken as a sign of how far the government had become detached from the people. A series of sit-ins and boycotts of university classes quickly followed. *The People's Daily*, the official CCP newspaper, raised the temperature by denouncing all this as the work of 'a small handful of plotters' who must be crushed immediately.

I If we are tolerant of, or conniving with, this disturbance and let it go unchecked, a seriously chaotic state will appear. Then, the reform and opening up; the improvement of the economic environment and the rectification of the economic order, construction, and development; the
5 control over prices; the improvement of our living standards; the drive to oppose corruption; and the development of democracy and the legal system expected by the people throughout the country, including the young students, will all become empty hopes. Even the tremendous achievements scored in the reform during the past decade may be
10 completely lost, and the great aspiration of the revitalisation of China cherished by the whole nation will be hard to realise. A China with very good prospects and a very bright future will become a chaotic and unstable China without any future.

Aroused rather than deterred by such threats, students from over 40 universities in China joined their fellows in Tiananmen Square. A particularly ominous portent for the government was the solidarity the transport workers showed with the students by allowing them to travel to Beijing without paying their fares. Zhao Ziyang, the Party General Secretary, tried to appease the protesters by making a public statement in which he suggested that *The People's Daily* had gone too far. But the demonstration in Tiananmen Square had begun to develop a momentum. By the second week of May a group of three hundred students had gone on hunger strike. For the first time the government made direct contact with student representatives, urging them to call off the strike. A number of China's leading writers added their voice to this appeal but at the same time pleaded with the Government to recognise the protest as a genuinely democratic and patriotic movement.

The students declined to abandon their protest because they

believed that events had given them two advantages that they could exploit. The first was the wide international media coverage that they were receiving; foreign camera crews and journalists from every continent had taken up residence in the Square. Even if the Chinese government could disregard the effect this would have in China, since Chinese television broadcasts carried very little reference to the crisis in Beijing, it could not so easily discount the second supposed advantage. Student leaders calculated that the government's hands were tied by the imminent arrival in Beijing of Mikhail Gorbachev, the first Russian leader to be invited to China since the Sino-Soviet rift. His visit explained the presence of the world's press in Beijing. The students revered Gorbachev as the progressive leader of a socialist state who was introducing into his country the very reforms that they were demanding for China. They believed that while he was present in China the government would not dare to crush their demonstration.

The visit of Gorbachev, which began on 16 May, may have indeed delayed the authorities taking firm action but their anger at having to change his schedule and itinerary made the hardliners still more resolute against the protesters. With Tiananmen Square now occupied by rebellious students the plan to impress Gorbachev with the type of

Protesters put up a wall poster calling for 'Glasnost' (open government), 1989

organised mass rally that Khrushchev had witnessed on his visit in 1959 had to be curtailed. The talks between the Soviet and Chinese leaders did go ahead but in a strangely unreal atmosphere. What should have been a historic Sino-Soviet summit had been overshadowed. The truly historic events were happening elsewhere in Beijing.

6 The Tiananmen Square Massacre, June 1989

On 19 May, the sixth day of the hunger strike and the day that Gorbachev left China, Zhao Ziyang again went down to the Square to address the students. In obvious distress, he promised them that the issues over which they were protesting would eventually be resolved. Li Peng also spoke to the students briefly, but his was a perfunctory visit; it seems that he and Deng Xiaoping had already decided that the demonstrations were to be ended by force. It was this that gave particular poignancy to Zhao's parting words to the students, 'I came too late, too late ... We are too old to see the day when China is strong. But you are young. You should stay alive'. That same evening Zhao was dismissed from his post and Li Peng in a broadcast speech in which he condemned the students as 'rioters' formally declared the imposition of martial law.

1   The situation in Beijing is still developing, and has already affected many
    other cities in the country. In many places, the number of demonstra-
    tors and protesters is increasing. In some places, there have been many
    incidents of people breaking into local party and government organs,
5   along with beating, smashing, looting, burning, and other undermining
    activities that seriously violated the law. Some trains running on major
    railway lines have even been intercepted, causing communications to
    stop ... All these incidents demonstrate that we will have nationwide
    major turmoil if no quick action is taken to turn and stabilize the situa-
10 tion. Our nation's reforms and opening to the outside world, the cause
    of the four modernizations, and even the fate and future of the People's
    Republic of China, built by many revolutionary martyrs with their blood,
    are facing a serious threat.

The news of the government's intention to apply 'firm and resolute measures to end the turmoil' rallied the students who had begun to waver. They voted to end the hunger strike but to continue their occupation of the Square. It is arguable that this is what the hardliners in the government wanted. Were the demonstrators to have peacefully dispersed at this point it would have deprived the authorities of the chance to make an example of them. But things did not go entirely the government's way. When news of the demonstrators' determination to stay in the Square became known, thousands who had earlier given up now returned, their numbers swollen by the ordinary citizens of Beijing. It was these Beijing residents who blocked the roads and avenues leading to Tiananmen and prevented the first wave of troops, sent to impose martial law, from reaching the Square. The troops were bewildered by this show of popular resistance. After discussions with the leaders of the demonstration their commanders ordered their men to withdraw to the outskirts of the city.

But this proved to be the lull before the storm. With Zhao removed and Li Peng and Deng now prepared to exercise full authority, the plans for ending the protest were activated. Crack troops led by commanders specially appointed by President Yang Shangkun and Deng Xiaoping advanced on Beijing. By 2 June 350,000 PLA soldiers had surrounded the Square and had secured the routes leading to it. This time the troops were not to be deterred by the pleas of the local people. The commanders defined the PLA's action as a 'full military campaign' to overcome the determined resistance of the 'rebels' occupying Tiananmen Square, which the troops were instructed to reclaim 'at all costs'. Tanks and armoured personnel carriers rumbled into position. At 10 pm on the night of 3 June the first shots were fired into the demonstrators. Shooting continued intermittently through the hours of darkness and into the morning. By mid-day on 4 June the occupation was over. The scene was one of carnage. Twisted barricades crushed by the PLA tanks lay strewn around, mixed with the

A lone man halts a line of tanks as they approach Tiananmen Square, June 1989 - he was pulled away, but it is not known what became of him

accumulated garbage of the six-week occupation. At regular intervals, lines of exhausted, injured, and broken-spirited students were marched away for interrogation and imprisonment.

The number of dead and injured will probably never be fully known but estimates suggest that, including the people killed in the surrounding streets and the PLA soldiers attacked by outraged crowds, the figure ran into thousands. Despite the news blackout that the government immediately imposed, the information that leaked out regarding the number of victims treated in Beijing's hospitals confirmed that a massacre had indeed occurred. In the following weeks demonstrators who had escaped from Tiananmen but had not been able to flee the country were rounded up. Reprisals followed. Those identified as ringleaders were given stiff prison sentences. CCP officials who had shown sympathy for the protesters were dismissed for their wrong-headedness, while those who had resisted the demonstrators were promoted for their loyalty to the Party.

Looking at the Tiananmen protest in relation to the powers at the government's disposal, commentators have suggested that the demonstration could have been dispersed by organised police armed with no more than water cannon and tear gas. This was the normal way in which student riots were dealt with in Asian countries. The students were unarmed and far from united over how long their protest could be sustained. It would not have taken much to scatter them. It is difficult, therefore, to avoid the conclusion that Deng and the Chinese leaders wanted a violent end to the affair. For their two-month defiance of the government, the protesters were to be made to atone in blood. The resort to tanks and bullets was intended to impress upon the Chinese both the seriousness of the demonstrators' challenge to civil order and the determination of the government not to tolerate such rebellion. The massacre in Tiananmen was very much in the Chinese tradition of crushing opposition by the severest means in order to emphasise the illegitimacy of opposition itself. It was the clearest sign yet that the post-Mao liberalisation did not include an extension of political freedoms. The CCP might be willing to consider its own internal reform. What it would not contemplate was giving up its authority over the Chinese nation.

Studying 'China After Mao: The Deng Era'

Three key linked themes can be identified in the chapter on Deng's China: 1. The Third Plenum, 1978; 2. Deng's revolution; 3 The pro-democracy movement

1. The Third Plenum, 1978

Key Question: Why did the Third Plenum of 1978 prove to be a landmark in the development of the PRC?

Section 2 of this chapter is the obvious required reading but it is also necessary to study Section 3 as this is where the ramifications of the Third Plenum are described.

Points to Consider: Clearly it is important that you define 'landmark' in this context. Working definitions might be - 'new departure', 'turning point', a 'critical period of adjustment'. Any one of these metaphors would provide a useful reference point for your analysis. It would also help considerably if you were to explain that the Third Plenum was a specially convened meeting of the CCP's policy-making body - the Central Committee. A major point to be stressed is the Third Plenum's adoption of the Deng's 'four modernisations' programme. It was on this that China's economic structure was to be rebuilt. Another vital decision to refer to is the acceptance of 'the one country, two systems' formula. Although this was initially conceived as a possible means of resolving the Taiwan and Hong Kong issues, you would do well to point out its implications for China's internal economy - it offered the opportunity that was subsequently taken up of running a capitalist economy in parallel with a socialist political system. A sub-question you could ask yourself is whether the Third Plenum was as significant politically as it was economically. The resolution on party democracy finally removed the shadow of the Cultural Revolution, allowing the rehabilitation of Deng Xiaoping and his chief supporters. Factors and details such as these provide plentiful support for arguing that the Third Plenum had momentous consequences for the PRC.

2. Deng's Revolution

Key Question: Do the reforms introduced under Deng Xiaoping after 1978 merit the description 'revolution'?

The whole of Chapter 4 is relevant, with Section 3 clearly being of the most value. It would also be worth rereading section 2d in Chapter 1 and Section 2 in Chapter 7.

Points to Consider: The key term is obviously 'revolution' and although its meaning may be thought obvious you would be well advised to begin by defining the term. In this context it may be taken to mean a complete break from previous Maoist policies. The Central Committee's 1981 resolution declaring that Mao had made serious errors allows the suggestion to be made that this was the prelude to the introduction of major change. Although it is necessary to give some details of the actual shifts in agricultural and industrial strategy, it is also important to point that the revolution was equally concerned with inculcating a new attitude among the Chinese. The fact that, in the matter of economic planning, utility and practicality were to replace dogma and that talent was to be given its head was a remarkable change of attitude. You should consider just how striking a break with Maoist practice Deng's opening up China to the world was. It involved the pursuit of harmonious international relations and the acceptance of China's need to introduce capitalist methods in order to make itself genuinely competitive industrially and commercially. However, while Deng's economic reforms may well be classed as revolutionary, your answer would lack balance if you did not indicate the differences between Deng's economics and his politics. In political affairs Deng was insistent that no major changes should be made. For the sake of China's stability he refused to contemplate the CCP's loosening its grip on the nation. The absolutism of the Party had to be preserved. This curious mixture of economic progressivism and political reaction suggests that Deng's reforms might be better termed 'the partial revolution' or 'China's unfinished revolution'.

3. The pro-democracy movement

Key Question: Did the pro-democracy movement of the 1980s ever have a realistic chance of succeeding?

All sections of Chapter 3 are relevant; reference should also be made to Section 2c of Chapter 1.

Points to Consider: The critical question is 'succeeding' in what? It is vital that you begin by describing what the democrats' aims actually were. A good starting point would be Deng's four fundamentals. To these, which were essentially a set of arguments against change, the democrats wished to add a fifth - democracy - by which they meant not only greater electoral participation but also the curbing of government corruption. It is worth stressing that during its early development at the beginning of the 1980s the pro-democracy movement was not necessarily anti-government. But what the democrats never grasped was that for Deng and the CCP democracy was never an option. After the upheavals of the Cultural Revolution, the Party leaders considered that internal political stability was a paramount need. The government and pro-democrats had incompatible notions of what the term democracy meant. For the government the word meant democratic centralism which excluded popular participation. For the democrats it meant pluralism and the end of the CCP's monopoly of government. There was no middle ground of understanding. A point worth making is that the tradition and machinery of participatory democracy did not exist in China. The pro-democrats in China were a small, though educated and vocal, minority. The notion that the established CCP government, determined under Deng to preserve its authority, would willingly grant any real political concessions to them was always unrealistic. As the 1980s progressed this difference widened and relations became embittered, reaching a bloody climax in Beijing in 1989.

The following is an analysis of three related documents central to the theme of 'the Deng Era'. They relate to the suppression of the pro-democracy movement. These appear on pages 76, 78 and 80.

1 - Context

The first extract comes from a speech of Deng Xiaoping's following the government's crushing of the student protests of 1986. The second is from an editorial in *The People's Daily*, the government's official mouthpiece, condemning the Tiananmen incident of April 1989, which proved to be the first stage of the pro-democracy demonstration in Beijing in that year. The third is part of a speech by President Li Peng delivered in May in which he condemned the demonstration as a riot and declared martial law.

2 - Meaning

In the first extract Deng justifies the rule of the CCP in China. For him it is a practical question. China does have local democracy but it is such a vast country, with such a heterogeneous and under-educated population, that to hold elections at national level is an organisational impossibility. In ideological terms true democracy already exists in China in the form of 'democratic centralism', the rule of Communist Party which derives its authority from the will of the people as expressed in 'the system of people's congresses'. The critical statement is that reform must be based on socialist principles and that 'without the leadership of the Communist Party, there can be no building of socialism'. The second extract expresses the CCP's anger with the students occupying Tiananmen Square. By engaging in such anti-government behaviour the protesters are creating chaos and threatening the very reforms for which they claim to be demonstrating. Ominously, *The People's Daily* warns that the protest cannot be allowed to 'go unchecked'. Li Peng's statement in the third extract details the chaos and disruption caused by the pro-democracy student protesters. Li claims that the students are not merely undermining 'the cause of the four modernisations'; they are putting 'the future of the People's Republic of China' at risk.

3 - Significance

Together these extracts provide an explanation for the violent climax of the pro-democracy movement in 1989. It is clear from Deng's definitions that the CCP interprets democracy in a narrow party sense. Democratic centralism does not embrace the notion of full participatory politics in China for which the pro-democrats were demonstrating. The authority of the Party is absolute and must be obeyed. Reform is possible but only if led and directed by the Party. To protest against the Party is to challenge socialism which is the bedrock of the

Chinese nation. It is the notion that protest is fundamentally improper and therefore not permissible that informs the attitude of *The People's Daily* and Li Peng's statement. Very much in keeping with Chinese authoritarian tradition, the CCP under Deng and Li let it be known that the only response to continued defiance would be violent dispersal. What the sources combine to show is that Deng's Revolution was never intended by those in authority to betoken a relaxing of Party rule. Economic reform was not to be accompanied by political change.

Summary Diagram
China After Mao: The Deng Era

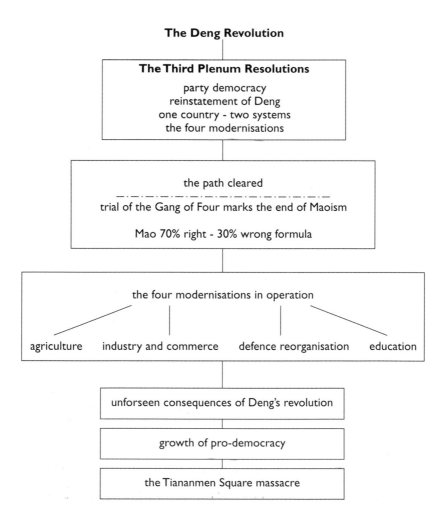

The Deng Revolution

The Third Plenum Resolutions
party democracy
reinstatement of Deng
one country - two systems
the four modernisations

the path cleared
trial of the Gang of Four marks the end of Maoism

Mao 70% right - 30% wrong formula

the four modernisations in operation

agriculture   industry and commerce   defence reorganisation   education

unforseen consequences of Deng's revolution

growth of pro-democracy

the Tiananmen Square massacre

5 China in the Wider World

1 The Character of the PRC's Foreign Policy

Some historians have gone so far as to suggest that Communist China did not really have a foreign policy in the orthodox sense that the older established nations had. Since it was often locked claustrophobically into its own domestic turmoil, it looked on the outside world as a distraction. Its response when it had to deal with foreign powers was invariably suspicious and aggressive. Its contempt for diplomatic conventions was evident at the height of the Cultural Revolution in the organised mob attack on the British Embassy in Beijing and the attack by machete-wielding Chinese Embassy staff on London policemen. Certainly the PRC did not operate by the traditional rules of international diplomacy. It showed itself extremely sensitive to real or imagined slights and was quite capable of breaking off diplomatic relations on the smallest pretext. The reverse side of this was that it often heaped disproportionate amounts of praise on those countries which were prepared to speak well of China. This also applied to individuals. Communist China's estimation of the worth of foreign politicians was based entirely on their value to China. Thus the Chinese lauded Richard Nixon, the US President from 1968 to 1973, and Edward Heath, the British Prime Minister between 1970 and 1974, as great international statesmen even though both leaders were regarded largely as failures in their own countries. It was enough in the eyes of the PRC that both men were perceived to be pro-Chinese.

Yet, orthodox or not in its conduct of foreign policy, Red China certainly had definable attitudes towards international affairs between 1949 and the 1990s. Three features are dominant: the PRC's fear of the USA, its rivalry with the USSR, and its wish to represent itself as the champion of the oppressed peoples of the world. In addition to these international concerns, much of the foreign policy of the PRC was shaped by its determination to consolidate what it regarded as its own territorial sovereignty. Immediately after it had taken power in 1949 the PRC began to consider how it could extend its authority over the whole of China. There were three areas that had traditionally been regarded by the Chinese as their territory but which in 1949 were outside China's control: Tibet, Taiwan and Hong Kong. (It should be stressed that although these are treated in this chapter as issues in China's foreign policy, the PRC consistently asserted that they were domestic matters since the regions were part of China's sovereign territory.) Tibet was rapidly occupied by the PLA (see page 106), but, before the PRC could begin the process of retaking Taiwan and Hong Kong, China was drawn into a protracted and exhausting war in Korea.

2 China and the Korean War, 1950-3

The Korean War proved to be a formative episode in the early development of the PRC. Between 1910 and 1945 the Korean peninsula had been occupied by the Japanese. After Japan's defeat in 1945 Korea was partitioned along the line of the 38th parallel of latitude; the USA took responsibility for protecting the part of the peninsula to the south of that line, with the Soviet Union playing an equivalent role in the region to the north. In 1950 the North Koreans crossed the parallel with the intention of establishing Communist control over the whole country. There have been various attempts to explain this move. It was once believed that the whole affair had been initiated by Mao in collusion with Stalin. This was the US State Department's interpretation at the time. Their sensitivity over the 'loss' of China to the CCP in 1949 led the Americans to assume that the Communist invasion of South Korea was the first joint venture of the new Communist bloc formed by Red China and the USSR. However, it is now known that Mao was as much taken by surprise by the North Korean move as were the Americans. Korea seems hardly to have been discussed at the Sino-Soviet meetings in Moscow in 1950 (see page 114). China's current military plans were exclusively concerned with Taiwan and Tibet. Indeed, apart from those two areas, the PRC had recently made the decision to cut back on military expenditure and redirect its resources into domestic projects.

What commentators now suggest is that Stalin had colluded with Kim Il Sung, the North Korean leader, in organising the invasion and that he called upon the Chinese to give support only after the fighting had started. Stalin was playing Cold War politics. Having been convinced by Kim that North Korea was capable of sustaining a major war effort against the Americans, Stalin calculated that the USA would be sucked into a conflict in Asia which it could not win. The great advantage as he saw it was that war in Korea entailed no risk to the USSR since Soviet forces would not be directly involved. This gave particular significance to the USSR's decision not to attend the vital meeting of the UN Security Council in June 1950 which voted to send UN forces to Korea. Historians used to believe that the USSR had miscalculated at this critical juncture by walking out of the Security Council in protest at the Western powers' recognition of Taiwan rather than the PRC as the true China. It was judged that the walk-out left the other four Security Council members (the USA, Britain, France, and Nationalist China) free to vote for the sending of a UN army to Korea, knowing that the USSR could not use its veto to block the resolution. However Andre Gromyko, the Soviet foreign minister, later admitted that the Soviet Union's decision to boycott the Security Council was a deliberate move by Stalin to entice the USA into the Korean conflict.

Mao's ignorance of Stalin's true intentions has led Jonathan

Spence to describe the PRC's involvement in the Korean War as 'a study in ambiguity'. The ambiguity arose from Mao's never having fully understood the situation; he remained in the dark regarding Stalin's motives. Stalin judged that if the North Koreans could take the South and thus bring the whole of Korea under Communist control, the benefits to the USSR would be considerable. The USA would have been humiliated and the Soviet Union would have acquired a very powerful position in the Far East at very little cost to itself. What helped in this was that under the Moscow agreement of 1950 China had ceded to the USSR the control of key naval stations and rail links in Manchuria. Furthermore, the PRC governor in Manchuria, Gao Gang, had already collaborated with Stalin in a number of secret agreements which effectively left Manchuria a vassal state of the Soviet Union. In the words of Harrison Salisbury, if South Korea could now be added to this list of Soviet advantages, 'Stalin's noose around north China and Beijing would be complete'.

Since he had not been a party to the plan devised by Stalin and Kim Il Sung, Mao was at first hesitant to commit China to the Korean struggle. But once he realised the affair was a *fait accompli* he felt obliged to enter. As a north-eastern neighbour Korea was too close geographically for China to remain detached. It was also the case that at this early stage in its development the PRC invariably followed the Soviet lead in international affairs. Yet Mao's views prevailed in China only after a battle with his leading military commanders. Gao Gang and Lin Biao argued that the PRC's primary task was to crush its internal enemies and that it did not have the resources to fight in Korea. Mao's counter argument was that once US troops had entered Korea it would be impossible for China to stay out; if the Americans were to take Korea they would possess a stepping stone to China itself.

The Western view of the Korean crisis was that it had been precipitated by the North Koreans when they crossed the 38th parallel and attacked the South. The PRC counter-claimed that the South Koreans had committed the initial aggression. When American forces under the UN flag landed in Korea in June 1950, Zhou Enlai condemned it as an imperialist invasion. Organised mass demonstrations took place in China's cities. The principal slogan was 'North Korea's friends are our friends. North Korea's enemy is our enemy. North Korea's defence is our defence'. Zhou warned that China would be forced to intervene if American troops pushed into North Korea. In fact thousands of PLA soldiers were already fighting alongside the North Koreans as 'volunteers'. In October 1950 US forces under General MacArthur crossed northwards over the 38th parallel. China promptly declared itself to be fully engaged in the war.

By the end of 1950 a quarter of a million PLA troops under the command of Peng Dehuai had moved into Korea. During the course of the ensuing three-year war that number was to run into millions.

Despite China's pretence that all its troops were volunteers it was a conscript army which fought in Korea. It suffered heavily in the fighting. When a truce was called in 1953 the PLA had lost nearly a million men (including Mao Zedong's oldest son, Mao Anying). This was the result of the deadly fire power that the UN aircraft and ground forces brought to bear on the Chinese troops who tended to attack fixed positions in concentrated numbers, a tactic that produced great deeds of heroism but appalling casualty figures.

The outcome of the Korean conflict suggested that Mao had been right in his initial reservations about Chinese involvement. The Panmunjom Amnesty in 1953 left Korea still divided and with no prospect of a Communist takeover in the south. A further consequence was that the USA pledged itself to the defence of Taiwan and to the continued support of Nationalist China's membership of the UN, a position that was maintained until 1972. In addition to the cost in Chinese lives, the Korean War was a huge drain on the young PRC's economy. Industrial resources earmarked for domestic growth had to be diverted into the war effort. The material losses incurred during the Korean conflict took more than a decade to make good.

These were obviously serious consequences, but the war did have some positive results for Communist China. The government's call for national unity to enable the PRC to surmount its first great crisis helped Mao and the CCP consolidate their hold over China by crushing the remnants of the GMD on the mainland. The three-year experience of war hardened China's resolve to stand alone in a hostile world. Furthermore, contrary to Stalin's original hopes, the Soviet Union's prestige had suffered. Although Stalin had encouraged the war, the USSR chose to play no direct military part. That had been left to the North Koreans and the Chinese. The sacrifices they made were prodigious. Mao proudly claimed that it was Chinese not Soviet comrades who had shed their blood in the cause of international Communism. Moreover, China's military successes in the war suggested that it need not fear the USA. Communist China had been able to achieve a military stalemate with the Americans in Korea, despite their nuclear capacity. The deep differences between the PRC and the USA which the war had emphasised were now a vital factor in international relations.

3 The PRC and the United States

a) The Roots of Sino-American Hostility

For a generation after 1949 relations between the PRC and the United States were tense and bitter. The specific reasons were not hard to find. America's anger at the 'loss of China' to Communism, the conflict in Korea, CIA involvement in Tibet, the USA's protection of Taiwan, its refusal to grant diplomatic recognition to the PRC, and the development of Chinese atomic weapons in the 1960s: these, taken together with the underlying ideological divide between the capitalist and Marxist systems they each represented, explain Sino-American animosity. From 1950 the PRC mounted a continuous campaign of vilification against 'American imperialism' which included the daily chanting by China's schoolchildren of the mantra 'Death to the American imperialists and all their running dogs'. The campaign reached new levels of intensity during the Cultural Revolution and the Vietnam War into which the USA was drawn in the late 1960s.

Although official Chinese Communist propaganda made great play of Mao Zedong's mockery of the USA as 'a paper tiger', Mao's public bravado belied his private disquiet. From the time of the Korean War onwards he was convinced that the USA was planning a retaliatory attack on China. There was a remarkable similarity between Joseph Stalin and Mao Zedong in this regard. They shared an abiding fear that their respective countries were in constant danger of a strike against them by Western forces. Mao calculated, as Stalin had done earlier in the USSR, that when the West was ready it would move to destroy Communism.

His anxieties led him to devise an internal defensive strategy for China, known as 'the Third Line'. This was a plan for a vast network of fortifications, installed above and below ground, so strongly built as to be capable of withstanding the heaviest bombardment, including atomic weapons. To organise this great defensive system Mao turned to Deng Xiaoping, who undertook the task with his customary dedication. Deng planned to use the existing bases, which had been created by the GMD during the war against Japan, to establish a series of industrial and military settlements that would be defensible against US airstrikes. The Third Line was to be located in the remoter regions of central China into which, in the event of an American attack, the population and industries of the vulnerable eastern and southern provinces could be withdrawn. Deng aimed to overcome the remoteness of the designated areas by creating a communication network capable of sustaining the projected military-industrial complex. As envisaged, the schemes entailed a massive reallocation of Chinese industry and labour. Although the Third Line was never fully completed, the many constructions that were finished became a model for the large-scale industrial projects which were later to provide the basis of Mao's economic strategy for China.

b) The Parting of the Bamboo Curtain

The Chinese fears that had led to the creation of the Third Line hardly suggested that there was any likelihood of an easing of Sino-American rivalry. Yet this is what began to happen in the early 1970s. A major factor was the USA's reversal of its position on Chinese representation in the United Nations; in 1971 it formally recognised Red China's

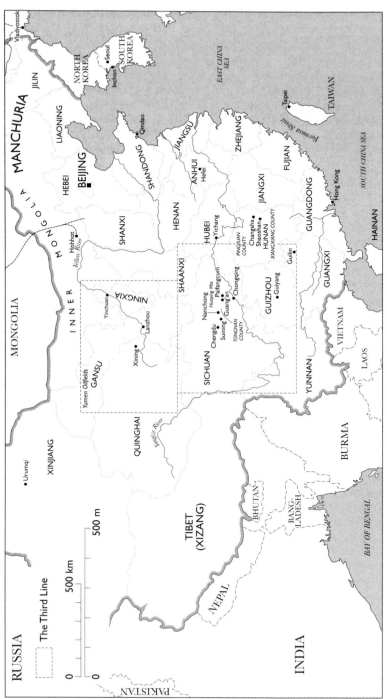

Map of China showing the Third Line

right to replace Taiwan in the UN (see page 95). This important diplomatic gesture encouraged the PRC to soften its approach to the USA. While Mao was alive, the fear that he had bred into the Chinese people of an American military attack would never entirely disappear, but in the aftermath of the USA's formal recognition of the PRC it was suspended sufficiently to allow talks to begin in 1971.

The initial diplomacy was conducted by Zhou Enlai and Henry Kissinger, the US President's special adviser on foreign affairs. A gesture that caught the headlines on both sides of the Pacific was the PRC's invitation to the US table-tennis team, then touring Japan, to play in China. It was this that gave the name 'ping-pong diplomacy' to the negotiations. The talks between Zhou and Kissinger prepared the way for President Nixon's visit to China in February 1972. Whatever the outcome of the visit might be, that it took place at all made it a momentous event. For the leader of the USA, 'the number one enemy nation', to be invited to China would have been unimaginable only a few years earlier. It is true that the talks between Nixon and Mao Zedong yielded little more than a few formal courtesies, but the accompanying discussions between Chinese and American diplomats were more productive. At the end of Nixon's visit a joint communiqué was issued in which the two nations expressed the hope that there would be continuing Sino-American contacts; the desirability of commercial, cultural and educational exchanges was emphasised. Both parties also agreed to give further consideration to ways in which the previously intractable Taiwan issue could be resolved.

The importance of Nixon's visit was more than merely symbolic. It had indicated that after the upheavals of the Cultural Revolution China was prepared to lift 'the bamboo curtain' and be more outward looking. It was a development that was to become much more marked in the post-Mao years when Deng Xiaoping's modernisation programme actively embraced the notion of China opening itself to the world. The Chinese were undoubtedly assisted in this by the more pliant attitude of the Americans. Sino-American rapprochement continued through the 1970s, reaching its highest point in 1979 with the establishment of full diplomatic relations between the two countries. In that year Deng Xiaoping accepted a presidential invitation to visit the USA where he made a favourable impression on the politicians and enthusiastic crowds who greeted him. Such events did not immediately wipe out the mutual suspicion engendered over long years of East-West hostility. Much remained to divide the two nations. But the machinery for diplomatic contact and trade was now in place.

What results all this would bring depended very largely on whether the two sides could settle their differences over what the PRC described as 'the crucial question obstructing the normalization of relations between China and the United States' - Taiwan.

c) The Taiwan Issue

In spite of the Truman Doctrine, issued in 1947, which committed the USA to giving direct support to free peoples resisting outside aggression, Taiwan had been initially excluded from the sphere of Far Eastern territories that the USA was prepared to defend. Early in 1950 President Truman had announced:

1   The United States has no desire to obtain special rights or privileges or to establish military bases on Formosa [Taiwan] at this time. Nor does it have any intention of utilizing its armed forces to interfere in the present situation. The United States Government will not pursue a
5   course which will lead to involvement in the civil strife in China.

Thus there seemed to be no chance of the USA's intervening to prevent Taiwan from being taken over by the mainland Chinese. But the seizure did not occur for two reasons. One was the military problem. The PLA judged that it did not possess the necessary air power and landing craft to mount a successful invasion of the well-defended island. The second reason arose directly from the Korean War. In their plans for fighting in Korea, US military advisers had insisted that the straits between Taiwan and the mainland and the strategically vital islands of Quemoy and Matsu (see the map on page 00) be neutralised to prevent their falling under Chinese Communist control. This led to the US Seventh Fleet being dispatched to patrol the area, and troops and weapons being sent to the Nationalists on Taiwan. The Americans were now pledged to protect Chiang Kaishek's island from Communist attack from the mainland.

This did not prevent Quemoy and Matsu being periodically shelled by PLA batteries, a tactic that the Communists kept up even after the Korean War was over. In 1958 the intensity of the shelling coincided with an ominous build-up of PLA troops to suggest that an all-out Chinese assault on Taiwan was imminent. US vessels were fired on in the Taiwan straits. The USA prepared for war. But no assault was mounted from the mainland. The fact was that Communist China was not in a position to invade Taiwan. The PRC's aggression had been a gesture intended to keep the atmosphere tense but not to risk war with America.

Throughout the 1960s the PRC continued to rattle the sabre over Taiwan and to denounce the USA for its 'imperialist hold' over the island. Beijing insisted that Taiwan was merely in a state of 'temporary detachment while Chiang Kaishek and his GMD rebel bandits hold the island'. The PRC pledged that at the earliest opportunity Taiwan would be liberated and incorporated into China proper. The PRC's anti-American outpourings were particularly fierce at the height of the Cultural Revolution. But with the lifting of the bamboo curtain in the early 1970s the opportunity arose for Sino-American contacts to be renewed. Taiwan was one of the major questions considered at the official talks that accompanied President Nixon's visit to China in 1972. In the communiqué that was published both sides defined their basic attitude. Beijing left no doubt as to where it stood, declaring:

1 The Government of the People's Republic of China is the sole legal government of China; Taiwan is a province of China which has long been returned to the motherland; the liberation of Taiwan is China's internal affair in which no other country has the right to interfere; and all US
5 forces and military installations must be withdrawn from Taiwan. The Chinese Government firmly opposes any activities which aim at the creation of 'one China, one Taiwan', 'One China, two governments', 'two Chinas', an 'independent Taiwan', or advocate that 'the status of Taiwan remains to be determined'.

In its section of the communiqué, the USA broadly accepted this line; it acknowledged that Taiwan was part of China and that a peaceful settlement could best be achieved by the Chinese people themselves. 'With this in mind, it affirms the ultimate objective of the withdrawal of all US forces and military installations from Taiwan'. This easing of tension could not have taken place had it not been preceded by an important shift in the USA's attitude towards Taiwan's diplomatic status. Since 1949 the Americans had resolutely continued to recognise Chiang's GMD republic as the legitimate China. This meant that Taiwan retained its place on the Security Council and that Red China was denied membership of the United Nations. With such American backing, Chiang Kaishek had continued to play the role of international statesman and spokesman of China. All this was changed when Taiwan lost its place on the Security Council and its membership of the UN in 1971.

For two decades since 1950 Red China had been lobbying the member states to recognise its claim over that of the GMD. By 1971 the shift in the balance of the UN allowed this to happen. The majority of new members who joined were Third World and non-aligned countries who tended to side with Beijing. In the crucial votes this bloc was able to defeat the pro-Taiwanese group, consisting largely of the Americans and their allies. The USA finally accepted the inevitable. It withdrew its traditional support from Chiang Kaishek and Free China, formally recognised Red China and accepted the PRC's right to replace Taiwan in the UN. The process was carried to its logical conclusion in 1979 when full diplomatic relations were established between the USA and the PRC. This major reversal of American post-war policy caused considerable divisions within the USA itself and appalled Taiwan whose people took to the streets in violent protest against the American betrayal.

4 Taiwan - The Other Republic of China

a) Economic and Political Development

The recurring international tension over Taiwan tended to obscure the remarkable developments on the island itself. Under the GMD, Taiwan was ultimately to achieve striking economic success. Yet Chiang Kaishek's rule of the island was neither liberal nor democratic. The GMD operated the same policies after 1950 that had characterised its rule on the mainland between 1937 and 1949. It called itself Free China, but repression of all forms of opposition remained the outstanding feature of its political system. The GMD's million-strong army enabled it to enforce its rule over both the indigenous Taiwanese and the Chinese settlers who had fled there from the mainland in the face of the Red Army's advance. If Nationalist China was less oppressive than its giant rival, the PRC, this was a matter of degree rather than of kind.

The big difference between the two Chinese republics was that Taiwan in 1949 enjoyed advantages denied to the mainland. As a comparatively small island Taiwan was easy to control and organise. Moreover, during its sixty-year occupation by the Japanese before 1945 it had experienced very considerable economic development based on a sound administrative system. The GMD inherited an economy that had marked potential for growth. This began to be achieved in the 1950s once the United States had decided to support Nationalist China as part of its Cold War policy in the Far East. In the Mutual Security Pact signed between the GMD government and the USA in 1954, the Americans committed themselves to defend Taiwan against outside attack. An economic aid programme was drawn up which provided Taiwan with dollars and resources until 1968. American companies expanded into the region, bringing with them industrial expertise and management skills. By the 1960s US dollar investments had helped to make Taiwan a major international market. Between 1953 and 1962 the island witnessed a sevenfold increase in the value of its industrial exports.

An Economic Comparison of Taiwan and the PRC			
	1952-60	1960-65	1965-72
Overall GNP			
Growth Rate			
PRC	6.0%	4.7%	5.7%
Taiwan	7.2%	9.6%	10.1%
Per capita			
Growth Rate			
PRC	3.6%	2.9%	3.3%
Taiwan	3.6%	6.4%	7.3%

When, in the 1970s, Taiwan lost both its place in the UN and its recognition by the USA there were fears that this would seriously damage its economy. It was thought that its diplomatic isolation might be followed by a decline in its international trade and commerce. The worries proved unfounded. Far from declining, Nationalist China accepted the challenge of surviving by its own efforts and entered into a period of rapid development. During the 1980s a combination of strong government direction and major foreign investment enabled it to develop a manufacturing industry that was highly successful in exploiting the world demand for electronic goods. By the 1990s Taiwan ranked alongside Hong Kong and Singapore as one of Asia's 'tiger economies'. In 1991 it was in a position to undertake a $300 billion six-year investment plan for the development of a high-tech transport and communications system.

This economic achievement was accompanied by equally significant political changes. The GMD remained in government but the rigidities of its one-party rule were gradually eased. The death of Chiang Kaishek in 1975 marked the beginning of a liberalising of Taiwanese politics. Chiang's successor, his son, Jiang Jingguo (Chiang Ching-kuo), made important moves towards greater local and national democracy. The State legislature and the municipal governments became more genuinely representative of the Taiwanese people. Of equal note was the lifting of martial law in 1986, after thirty-seven years in operation. It was a measure of how far democracy had advanced that on Jiang's death in 1988, he was succeeded as President by Lee Teng-hui, a native Taiwanese. It was during Lee's presidency that the GMD formally accepted that one-party rule was unconstitutional. Ironically, in 1991 in the first elections of the new multi-party system, the GMD was returned to office with an overwhelming majority.

b) The Sovereignty Issue

In regard to Taiwan's relations with the mainland, Lee Teng-hui maintained the GMD's traditional approach. He restated Taiwan's right to be regarded as the genuine government of the whole of China, rejecting the notion of an independent, isolated, Taiwan. However, he took a conciliatory line towards Beijing, declaring that Taiwan had no intention of 'using force as a means of seeking reunification'. What helped Lee was that increasing economic contact was being made between Taiwan and mainland China. Although this was unofficial, it was of major importance since it undermined the notion that China and Taiwan were irretrievably separated. This encouraged Deng Xiaoping in the 1980s to modify the hard line the PRC had expressed in the 1972 communiqué. Indeed, he appeared willing to reverse the idea that the PRC would never tolerate 'one China, one Taiwan'. In 1984 Deng declared: 'The main system in China must be socialism.

The one billion people on the mainland will continue to live under the socialist system, but a capitalist system will be allowed to exist in certain areas, such as Hong Kong and Taiwan.'

The tone of Deng's remarks was very much in accord with the 'nine-principles' presented by the PRC in 1981 which set out a programme for 'the return of Taiwan to the motherland for the peaceful reunification of China':

1. **1.** We propose that talks be held between the Communist Party of China and the Guomindang of China on a reciprocal basis.
   2. We propose that the two sides make arrangements to facilitate the exchange of mail, trade, air and shipping services, family reunions and
5 visits by relatives as well as academic and cultural exchanges.
   3. After the country is unified, Taiwan can enjoy a high degree of autonomy as a special administrative region.
   4. Taiwan's current socio-economic system will remain unchanged.
   5. People in authority in Taiwan may takes up posts of leadership in
10 national political bodies and participate in running the state.
   6. When Taiwan's local finances are in difficulty, the Central Government may offer subsidies as appropriate.
   7. For people of all nationalities and public figures in Taiwan who wish to settle on the mainland, we will guarantee that proper arrangements
15 will be made, that there will be no discrimination and that they will have freedom of entry and exit.
   8. We hope that industrialists and businessmen in Taiwan will invest in the mainland, and their legal rights, interests and profits will be guaranteed.
20 **9.** The reunification of the motherland is the responsibility of all Chinese.

At first sight these proposals seemed to suggest that the PRC was willing to concede on the crucial point of Taiwan's autonomy. But this was a misreading. Communist China may have softened its tone but on one essential it had not changed. Behind the more accommodating words there was the same resolution not to budge on the matter of the PRC's absolute right to govern the whole of China. Deng had made this clear in 1983:

1 We do not approve of 'complete autonomy' for Taiwan. There must be limits to autonomy, and where there are limits nothing can be 'complete'. 'Complete autonomy' means 'two Chinas', not one. Different systems may be practised, but it must be the People's Republic of China
5 that alone represents China.

Thus it was that, despite the better relations that had emerged between Taiwan and the mainland in the 1980s, the basic position remained unchanged; neither side was prepared to concede any substantial ground on the issue of sovereignty. Moreover, whatever harmony had developed was shattered by the events in Tiananmen Square in June 1989. Of what worth, the Taiwanese asked, were Beijing's fine words and promises when set against its willingness to destroy its own people?

In the 1990s the PRC and Taiwan, each in its separate way, remained wholly dedicated to the notion that it was the legitimate China. They both wanted reunification but they had totally contrary understandings of what that meant. The PRC had recovered Hong Kong in 1997. That success inspired the Chinese Communists to believe that the return of Taiwan was also possible. Deng Xiaoping's formula, 'one nation, two systems', had been invoked to ease the transition from British colonial rule to rule from Beijing. Deng believed that it could be applied equally to Taiwan. But that begged the question of sovereignty. China had been able to re-establish its right to Hong Kong because in the end the existing ruling power, Britain, accepted the legality of the PRC's claim to sovereignty. As things stood in the late 1990s the possibility that the government of Nationalist China would do the same appeared extremely remote.

5 The PRC and Hong Kong

The process by which the British colony of Hong Kong reverted to Chinese control in 1997 provides an illuminating insight into Communist China's perception of itself as a world power.

a) The Growth of Hong Kong

A key point to stress is that Hong Kong colony consisted of three distinct areas - Hong Kong island, Kowloon, and the New Territories. In 1842, in the Treaty of Nanjing, imposed on China after its defeat by the British in the Opium War, the Qing dynasty was forced to cede the island of Hong Kong to Britain in perpetuity. Eighteen years later in the Beijing Convention of 1860 the Qing government granted Britain, again in perpetuity, Kowloon harbour directly facing Hong Kong. In 1898 Britain took over the rest of Kowloon peninsula. This fresh acquisition, known as the New Territories, was ceded not in perpetuity but on a ninety-nine year lease. The British Crown Colony of Hong Kong so formed in 1898, was to develop during the following century into one of the most prosperous cities in the world.

It was in the second half of that period that its phenomenal growth occurred. In 1949 the status of Hong Kong as a British outpost within China gave it an obvious attraction to those fleeing from the Communist takeover of the Chinese mainland. It became a haven for thousands of businessmen and bankers who brought their wealth with them. Many came from Shanghai, hitherto the richest area of China. They became the entrepreneurs of Hong Kong, developing new lines of manufacturing based on shrewd estimates of the needs and tastes of a growing world market and achieved at low cost by the unscrupulous use of cheap refugee labour. In the 1970s a booming tourist industry added to the island's burgeoning wealth. Despite a brief recession in the mid 1980s, when the city's financiers suffered a temporary crisis of confidence, Hong Kong continued its economic growth. Such was the demand for land in an increasingly overcrowded area that a property boom occurred in the 1980s, helping to create a new class of 'super-rich' financiers. It was they who began to invest in Shenzen, the region that adjoined the New Territories and was one of PRC's Special Economic Zones. This was an extension of the process that had been going on for some time, but which Beijing was reluctant to admit, of mainland China benefiting directly from Hong Kong's wealth.

b) The Sino-British Problem

Hong Kong's economic miracle was both a reproach and an inspiration to China's Communist rulers. The city's capitalist success contrasted sharply with the low growth rate of socialist China. Yet at the same time it offered the prospect of the PRC's acquiring 'the pearl of the orient'. In 1997 China was due to inherit a dynamic

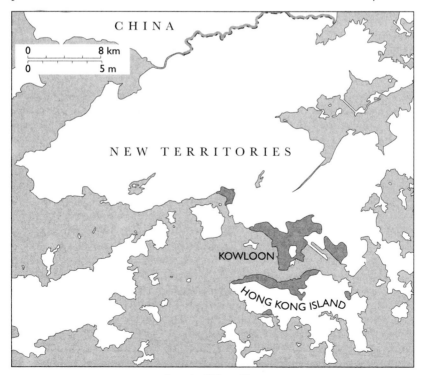

A map of Hong Kong

commercial city, which promised to provide a spectacular means of fulfilling Deng Xiaoping's programme for opening China's trade to the world.

But would Britain ultimately be willing to hand over the colony to what it regarded as a repressive regime? What the Chinese government feared was that the British would insist on retaining Hong Kong island in accordance with their entitlement under the original Nanjing Treaty. To Beijing's surprise, it was Britain which made the first significant move to resolve the question. The Sino-British talks on Hong Kong, which had begun in a somewhat desultory manner in 1979 became more focused in 1982 with the visit of Margaret Thatcher, the first British Prime Minister to go to China. There have been suggestions that her eagerness to reach a settlement played into Beijing's hands. It helped the PRC, which had been unsure about what diplomatic line to adopt, to begin the negotiations from a position of strength. Britain's formal legalistic approach enabled the Chinese to make the matter of sovereignty the central issue. The PRC adopted an uncompromising stance; it would settle for nothing less than the full restitution of China's ownership of Hong Kong. Thatcher was informed by Deng Xiaoping that there was no question of Britain's leasehold being extended; 'I would rather see Hong Kong torched than leave Britain to rule it after 1997', he told her.

It is important to appreciate the thinking that inspired Deng's anger. It was true that the original treaties appeared to give Britain a case for retaining Hong Kong and Kowloon even after the return of the New Territories to China in 1997. But such legal technicalities merely irritated the Chinese whose basic view was that the treaties were invalid since they had been originally wrung from a weak Qing government, unable to resist Britain's aggressive imperialism. The PRC reasserted that Hong Kong was an 'integral part of the Chinese nation' regardless of the claims of imperialist Britain, which had originally acquired the colony only through coercion. As The People's Daily put it: 'One hundred and fifty years ago, to maintain its drug trafficking in China, Britain launched the aggressive Opium War against China, during which it carried out burning, killing, rape, and plunder on Chinese soil.'

Sharp though the exchanges between Deng and Thatcher were, they did help to open the way for further formal Sino-British discussions. These were often strained affairs; there was clearly a wide gap in the understanding of political and legal principle between the two sides. But eventually a compromise was reached in the form of the Sino-British Joint Declaration, signed by Zhao Ziyang and Margaret Thatcher in December 1984. The British agreed that when the lease on the New Territories expired in 1997 sovereignty over the whole Hong Kong area would revert to the PRC. On their side the Chinese Communists made a commitment to leave the economic structure of the territory substantially unaltered; Hong Kong would remain a capitalist 'Special Administrative Region' (SAR) until 2047. Deng Xiaoping neatly defined the arrangement whereby communism and capitalism would co-exist in separate parts of China as 'one country, two systems'. It was a concept that could also be extended to Taiwan.

1 When we speak of two systems, it is because the main part of China, with a population of one billion, is practising socialism. It is under this prerequisite that we allow capitalism to remain in a small part of the country. This will help develop our socialist economy, and so will the
5 policy of opening to the world.

The system as it would apply to Hong Kong was defined in the Basic Law, which guaranteed that the post-1997 constitution would provide 'a high degree of autonomy'. The agreements reached gave promise of a smooth transition towards Chinese rule of Hong Kong. However, in June 1989 everything was thrown into doubt by the news of the Tiananmen Square massacre. The obvious question arose: if the PRC could shoot down its own people in its own capital of what value were the promises it had given regarding Hong Kong? From that moment on relations between Britain and Communist China grew increasingly strained as the time for the 1997 handover approached.

Matters became sharply personalised with the appointment in 1992 of Christopher Patten as the last British Governor of Hong Kong. Patten made it his aim to create a 'through train', that is to establish as much democracy as possible in Hong Kong before Britain's departure so that the incoming Communist administration would find representative institutions already in place. Beijing reacted furiously; it accused Patten of breaking faith by intruding into matters that lay solely within the jurisdiction of the PRC. His attempt to resurrect the plan to introduce a number of elected seats into Hong Kong's Legislative Council (LegCo), which hitherto had been solely an appointed body, was condemned as a piece of neo-imperialism aimed at embarrassing the PRC and creating instability in Hong Kong. Beijing let it be known that as soon as it took over it would replace Patten's LegCo with its own Nominated Legislative Council which would not include any members of the Hong Kong Democratic Party.

The PRC's bitterness was understandable. It was undeniable that Britain was only a belated convert to democracy in Hong Kong. During its previous 150 year administration it had made no attempt to introduce the representative principle into its government of the colony. All public positions had been filled by British appointees, not elected spokesmen of the Hong Kong people. Patten's programme for turning LegCo into a representative body was a sop to Hong Kong democrats and, as Beijing was quick to point out, it contradicted the 1984 Joint Declaration.

Patten was not helped by the critical response of former British negotiators, who accused him of adopting policies that undermined the achievements of thirteen years of patient Sino-British diplomacy.

The democrats in Hong Kong came to Patten's defence. They had already been embittered by Britain's refusal to grant more than a token number of British passports to the Hong Kong Chinese, to be used as a possible line of escape after 1997. They felt increasingly let down by what they regarded as Britain's line of least resistance towards Beijing. Even after Tiananmen Square had revealed the ruthlessness of the PRC in crushing dissidence, China continued to be accorded all the niceties of diplomatic protocol. John Walden, a former director of home affairs in the Hong Kong government, claimed that the reason for Patten's unpopularity with British diplomats was that in trying to extend democracy he revealed all too clearly that the policy previously followed by British officials had been one of surrender:

1   In the four years between 1986 and 1990, the Governor [Sir David Wilson], the Foreign Office and the British Embassy in Beijing played out a charade of deplorable dishonesty to cover up the fact that they were not implementing Parliament's requirement that representative govern-
5   ment be actively developed in Hong Kong before it was handed over. Far from it. What they were actually doing was secretly making concessions to Beijing.

Critics of the British mode of withdrawal form Hong Kong explained its unsatisfactory nature by reference to Britain's wish not to jeopardise its potential trade with a nation of over a billion people. The argument ran that it was economic considerations that dictated Britain's soft line towards Beijing, not only over Hong Kong but on a broader diplomatic front. An example was Margaret Thatcher's decision in 1990 not to meet the Dalai Lama lest it offend Beijing. The Western powers' relations with the PRC certainly compromised their moral standing. Rather than the question of human rights, it was thoughts of the potential Chinese market that determined Western policy towards the PRC.

In the end, the West adopted what the US State Department defined as a policy of 'engagement without endorsement'. This was really a euphemism to explain why the West was willing to continue trading and negotiating with the PRC while keeping its reservations about the human rights record of the Beijing regime. There were prominent spokesmen in the West who became apologists for the PRC. Edward Heath, a former British Prime Minister and one of the first Western statesmen to visit China after the lifting of the bamboo curtain in the early 1970s, even argued that the different histories of China and the West made it inappropriate to judge the two cultures by the same political standards. He suggested that it was unrealistic to expect Beijing to apply Western forms of democracy in Hong Kong or any other of its territories. Heath's was precisely the type of reasoning that offended the island's democratic parties who argued that it exemplified Britain's attempt to keep its conscience clear while selling out the Hong Kong people to a repressive regime.

At the time of the 1997 handover, just how repressive that regime would prove to be remained an open question. Commercial logic suggested that the PRC would be best advised to leave the ex-colony's economic system untouched so as to further the policy of opening China to the world. In the late 1990s, the signs were that the PRC's consciousness of its inheritance had led it to put economics before ideology and to implement in Hong Kong Deng Xiaoping's essentially pragmatic concept of 'one nation, two systems'.

6 The PRC and Anti-Colonialism

Ever since its creation in 1949 the PRC had regarded itself as the great model of successful resistance to imperialism. As its relations with the Soviet Union deteriorated, the PRC became progressively assertive in its claim that Maoist China not the revisionist USSR was the voice of proletarian revolution (see page 118). The PRC believed that this gave it a special role and duty to foment international subversion. Its self-proclaimed task was to lead those countries which had just gained independence or were still struggling against colonial rule to follow the Maoist path. The obvious areas were South-East Asia, the Middle East, Africa and Latin America. Chinese policy, therefore, developed two inter-connecting lines: to oust the Soviet Union from the leadership of international revolution and to undermine Western imperialism by supporting anti-colonialist movements throughout the world.

The architect of the PRC's policy towards the emerging nations was Zhou Enlai. A loyal Maoist and a veteran of the Long March, Zhou first came to prominence as China's representative when he skilfully negotiated the truce that brought the Korean war to an end in 1953. His growing reputation as a statesman of world rank led to his being invited to the Bandung Conference in 1955. This was a critical step in China's thrust to become the champion of the emerging nations. The Bandung meeting had been convened largely in response to the creation under American direction of SEATO (the South-East Asia Treaty Organisation), a collection of anti-Communist states. In contrast, the twenty-nine Asian and African states who gathered at Bandung used the occasion to assert their neutrality in a world that was rapidly dividing into the two armed East-West camps of the Cold War. India's leader, Jawaharlal Nehru, was impressed by the manner in which Zhou argued that it was the USA's aggressive stance that was the greatest challenge to world peace. Nehru hailed Zhou as a major statesman and depicted the PRC as the voice of liberated Asia.

Yet able and internationally renowned though Zhou Enlai was, the PRC largely failed in its twin aims of dominating international Communism and of leading the ex-colonial world. It is true that in the early 1990s the PRC did become the world's largest Marxist state. But that was a matter of default, the Soviet Union having disintegrated in 1991. Before then during its 40 year ideological struggle with the USSR, Communist China had succeeded in gaining the allegiance of only one European country, and that arguably the least significant - Albania (see page 120). The PRC fared little better in its efforts elsewhere. A basic reason for this was that China simply lacked the necessary economic and military resources. The greater part of China's claim to be guiding the forces of anti-colonialism was bluff and bravado. China did not have the wherewithal to be involved actively in more than a few selected areas. For example, it had little direct influence on Latin America. Some of the revolutionary organisations there did espouse Maoism, an outstanding example being the 'Shining Path' guerilla movement in Peru. But sheer distance and lack of resources prevented the PRC from offering much more than token assistance to subversion in South America. It was the same story in the Middle East. Despite the PRC's dabbling in the Arab-Israeli conflict by backing those states which were hostile to the West, Communist China was no more than an irritant in the proceedings. While the PRC did possess nuclear weapons after 1964, its lack of a sophisticated weapons-delivery system made its superpower status notional rather than real.

In addition to its limited resources, there were three other main reasons for the failure of China to impress the non-aligned and emerging nations - its expatriate problem, its policy in Tibet, and the impact internationally of its Cultural Revolution.

a) China's Expatriate Problem

It had been a consistent feature of Asian history for large numbers of Chinese to live and work in other Asian countries. This pattern continued after 1949. Rather than integrate into the local culture, the Chinese settlers tended to regard themselves as a discrete group whose first loyalty was to the PRC. This was encouraged by Beijing which granted its expatriates full Chinese citizenship. The result was particularly evident in Indonesia and Burma. In any dispute that those countries had with the PRC the Chinese expatriates took the side of the PRC and became a source of subversion. Similarly, in Malaya during the 'emergency' of the 1950s, the period of armed struggle against British rule, the independence movement was overwhelmingly composed of Chinese Communists. The pro-British Malay government claimed that these insurgents were organised and financed by the PRC. Beijing's standard defence to such charges was to assert that wherever Chinese nationals had settled in Asian countries they were subject to persecution by the host population. In 1959 there was certainly a massacre of Chinese in Indonesia when the local people turned on them, killing thousands and destroying their property. The basic cause had been Indonesian anger at the Chinese dominance of local businesses and trade. The resentment aroused in many

Asian countries by the presence of large numbers of Chinese was intensified at the time of the Cultural Revolution when Maoist fanaticism made the expatriates a highly volatile and disruptive element.

The arrogant behaviour of the Chinese settlers abroad, who often expressed contempt for their hosts, seriously compromised China's self-proclaimed role as the liberator of oppressed peoples. But the greatest damage to its reputation arose from its policy towards Tibet. It is this that provides the second main explanation for its limited success in attracting international support.

b) The PRC and Tibet

By a bitter irony the severity with which China asserted its control over the Tibetan people recalled the worst excesses of the colonialism against which it claimed to be struggling. In 1950 a PLA army was sent into Tibet to achieve 'reunification'. The PRC claimed that the region belonged historically to China. This was an assertion, not a statement of fact. The Tibetans were markedly different in race, culture and religion from the Chinese. Within six months the PLA had overcome the determined but hopeless struggle of the Tibetans. The region was renamed Xizang, protesters were rounded up, and a reign of terror was imposed. There was little response from the major powers. Britain was not prepared to intervene since its traditional interest in Tibet as a buffer state protecting India against Russian expansion had waned with the granting of Indian independence in 1947. Nor was the USA, whose defined spheres of interest in the Far East did not include Tibet. For its part, the USSR let it be known that it would allow China a free hand in Tibet provided that the PRC recognised Soviet claims to Mongolia.

Having gained control of the region, the Chinese initiated a prolonged campaign to destroy the Tibetan identity. The area was deliberately flooded with Han settlers in order to swamp the indigenous community. Local culture, religion and tradition were undermined by the aggressive imposition of a Chinese life-style. Despite their desperate position in the face of overwhelming Chinese military strength, the Tibetans maintained a continuous resistance over the next four decades. This defiance was invariably met with savage reprisals. It was a consistent and well-founded Chinese claim that the bulk of the resisters were trained by Central Intelligence Agency (CIA), America's anti-communist espionage organisation. In 1959 in the wake of particularly bitter Tibetan reaction against the Chinese occupation the PLA began a systematic assault on Tibet's Lama (Buddhist) religion. Monasteries were destroyed and nuns and priests were assaulted.

These outrages occasioned the flight of the Dalai Lama, the Tibetan spiritual leader. In 1959, he chose to leave the country rather than wait for his inevitable removal by the Chinese. He calculated that as an exiled but free man he would be better able to voice the plight of the Tibetan people to the outside world. In exile the Dalai Lama became a potent symbol of Tibetan resistance. It was through him that the world's media were kept informed of the continuing severity of the PLA's occupation.

The PRC's treatment of Tibet aroused worldwide condemnation, and not merely from the Western nations. China's claim that Tibet was purely an internal affair was a weak argument that certainly did not convince its western neighbour, India. In theory China's relations with India ought to have been amicable. Both nations had recently emerged from the shadow of foreign domination; the achievement of Indian independence from Britain in 1947 was as momentous as the creation of the PRC in 1949. Yet Sino-Indian relations were to be subject to constant strain. India was one of the first nations to recognise the PRC and Nehru initially had been greatly impressed by Zhou Enlai's conduct of Chinese foreign policy. But India had reacted anxiously when the Chinese Communists took over Tibet in 1950. The boundary between Tibet and India had been drawn by Britain in 1913, an arbitrary decision that China had never accepted. The Indians under Nehru were worried by the extent of the PRC's territorial claims in its newly-conquered province. In 1956 the Chinese began constructing a major roadway fifty miles into Indian territory. Sino-Indian border clashes continued throughout the 1950s as the PLA, extending its control over Tibet, established military positions on Indian soil. Tensions were further heightened in 1959 when Nehru's government, in the face of angry protests from Beijing, granted sanctuary in India to the Dalai Lama. A full-scale Sino-Indian war eventually broke out in 1962 along the Himalayan border. The Indian forces came off worse in the bitter conditions. Liu Shaoqi boasted that 'China had taught India a lesson and if necessary would teach her a lesson again and again'. The Tibetan issue and the disputed border question remained unresolved and deeply compromised Sino-Indian relations in the ensuing decades.

In the 1970s there appeared to be some easing in China's occupation of Tibet. The Chinese urged the Tibetans to consider the benefits that the 'reunification' had brought them - the end of feudalism and the introduction of schools, hospitals, and a modern transport system. But these meant little to the majority of the Tibetan people. They saw the Chinese as foreigners bent on crushing the culture and tradition of the region. Tibetan frustration continued to express itself in sporadic but determined resistance. In 1985 the Tibetan refusal to celebrate the twentieth anniversary of the creation of what the Chinese called the Tibetan Autonomous Region (TAR) led to violent clashes. 1987 and 1989 were also years of particular unrest when anti-Chinese demonstrations threatened to become a full-scale national rising before being put down by the PLA.

The visits of the Dalai Lama to the world's major capitals were a key factor in drawing international attention to what was happening in his country. He described the Chinese in Tibet as being engaged in a policy of 'cultural genocide'. His dignity and serenity made him an impressive representative of the cause of Tibetan independence. The awarding of the Nobel Peace Prize to him in 1989 was a formal recognition of this. Not surprisingly, the award caused considerable embarrassment to Beijing. Deng Xiaoping had hoped that the Dalai Lama would end his self-imposed exile and return to Tibet, thereby conferring legitimacy on Chinese rule there. Deng was to be disappointed. In 1993 a major demonstration took place in Lhasa, the Tibetan capital, that proved to be the largest in China since the 1989 Tiananmen Square protest. Thousands of Tibetans were arrested by the PLA. Beijing ordered the total destruction of the remnants of Tibetan culture. The Panchen Lama, second in rank to the Dalai Lama, was seized by the Chinese and taken into 'protective custody'.

Details of the extent and brutality of the Chinese repression were presented to the United Nations by Tibetan refugees. Their belief was that such revelations had an inhibiting effect on the Chinese government. News of the uprising and its suppression reached the West by way of 'Asia Watch', an international organisation concerned with monitoring human rights abuses. The PRC under Deng Xiaoping showed a sensitivity to international opinion which it had never displayed in Maoist days. Although the Chinese authorities did not acknowledge the connection, there were a number of occasions in the 1990s when the release or more lenient treatment of gaoled dissidents in Tibet and in China coincided with their case being taken up by human rights groups in the West. These, however, were merely gestures, made in order to put China in a better light in the eyes of its international trading partners. It did not indicate a change of heart. There was no relaxing of the Chinese government's grip on its peoples.

c) The Impact of the Cultural Revolution

It was the Cultural Revolution that undermined Zhou Enlai's efforts to extend PRC influence to Africa. By the 1960s Zhou had made a significant impact as China's outstanding international statesman. His frequent travels and meetings with world leaders had given him a matchless experience of diplomacy. His subtlety and patience were in marked contrast to the bombast and aggression with which Beijing usually expressed itself. His many visits to the newly-independent countries in Africa resulted in a series of agreements in which the PRC undertook to provide material help. One major example was China's aid in the construction of the Tanzanian-Zambian railway. But what made much of this assistance suspect was the espionage and intrigue that often accompanied it. The accusation that the PRC had made against the Soviet advisers to China in the 1950s, that they were industrial and political spies, was now turned against China itself. The African states asserted that Chinese aid came at the price of political subordination. This charge had particular weight at the time of the Cultural Revolution when China demanded that the supremacy of Maoist thought be accepted by all those nations who wished to have dealings with China.

At the height of the hysteria generated by the Cultural Revolution, Zhou Enlai was declared politically suspect in China and forced to withdraw from government. Deprived of Zhou's experience and moderating influence in foreign affairs, the PRC lost much of the diplomatic ground that had been made under him. Paranoia dominated China's relations with the outside world. The British and the Indonesian embassies in Beijing were burned down and a number of other foreign embassies in China were besieged and their staffs insulted. The Chinese Foreign Ministry offices were occupied by rampaging Red Guards who in an orgy of destruction obliterated a vast collection of China's foreign office records. In such an atmosphere it became impossible for other countries, whether friendly or not, to conduct meaningful foreign policy with the Chinese. China's instability made its pretensions to lead the world's oppressed peoples look increasingly fanciful.

7 China's International Role Since 1989

In international terms, the remarkable thing about the Tiananmen Square massacre in 1989 was that it made little difference to China's standing as a nation. While the PRC's action brought worldwide condemnation, this was not translated into diplomatic isolation or economic sanctions. The two Western countries with the closest links to China maintained their existing policies. The USA was reluctant to do anything that might harm its increasingly lucrative trade links with China, while Britain, anxious not to antagonise the Chinese in the run-up to the Hong Kong transfer in 1997, confined its protests to words not actions.

In the early 1990s, it so happened that by a fortunate combination of international circumstances the PRC made a number of gains that required very little effort on its part. The new Russian government that emerged to replace the fractured USSR in 1991 was not in a position to maintain all its former foreign commitments. One area from which it withdrew was the Pacific rim. The Soviet naval base at Vladivostock was decommissioned. This coincided with the decision of the Americans not to renew the lease on their naval base in the Philippines. In the absence of a Japanese war fleet of any size, Communist China was left in a position of dominance over a large slice of the western Pacific. This seemed to give an added truculence to the PRC's approach to foreign affairs. Its Asian neighbours were made starkly aware of this in the dispute over the Spratly Islands, an area in the south China seas which was thought to be a likely source of oil. Malayasia, Indonesia, the Philippines and Vietnam were all geographically closer than China to the islands and had arguably stronger claims to them, but it was China which, on the flimsiest of historical evidence, claimed priority in the area. It backed its demands with force; in one incident Chinese warships sank two Vietnamese vessels. The naval force that the Chinese sent to the region included nuclear-armed submarines; it was a frightening indication of how far the PRC was prepared to go to assert its authority.

The fall of the Communist regimes in the USSR and its satellites ended the Cold War. This had the effect of destroying the old certainties that had determined international alignments since the end of the Second World War. China still officially espoused Marxist revolution but its first concern now appeared to be its status and development as a world power in its own right. Just as, at home, its economic planning was divorced from rigid political ideology, so, too, in foreign affairs China no longer felt constrained by considerations of dogma. Its interests dictated that it disregard the ideological differences that had previously marred its relations with the USA. Commercial advantage now demanded that it cultivate the American connection. There was equal readiness on the other side. In 1992 the US government conferred on China the status of 'most favoured nation', America's customary way of establishing closer relations with selected countries by granting them special commercial privileges. The remarkable feature was that the conferment did not have the usual strings attached to it. It was not made a condition of China's privileged trade status that it conform to American standards concerning human rights. The USA, like China, was prepared to adapt to the world as it was rather than as it would like it to be.

Summary Diagram
China in the Wider World

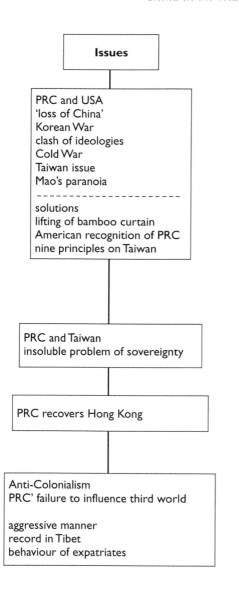

Conflicts

Korean War 1950-3

Sino-Indian war !965

PLA in Cambodia 1975

6 China and International Revolution

1 Background

The creation of the People's Republic of China was a second major victory for international Communism. In 1917 Russia had been the first great nation to undergo a successful Marxist revolution; China in 1949 was the second. The PRC's triumph left it with a dual purpose: to develop China into a modern nation and to lead the rest of the world towards international proletarian revolution. The pursuit of this second aim created huge questions for China. Was it realistic for an economically backward nation to attempt to play such a role? Would not an aggressive revolutionary attitude towards the capitalist world leave China friendless and unable to obtain essential resources? There was an equally difficult ideological question: where did the young PRC stand in the world Communist hierarchy? Was it merely to follow the Soviet Union? Since in historical terms the USSR was the senior revolutionary partner should its wishes be obeyed or did China have an equal right to interpret Marxism for itself? These were the questions which the new China struggled to answer in the second half of the twentieth century.

It has to be emphasised that the Chinese Communists did not regard Marxism simply as a political movement. For them it was a series of scientific truths. The task of the revolutionary was to discover these truths and then forcibly reconstruct society in accordance with them. This belief put Communism very much on a par with dogmatic religion. It had the same preoccupation with defining the truth about the human condition and with creating an unchallengeable ortho- doxy of belief. Just as all the major dogmatic faiths - Judaism, Christianity and Islam - splintered into fiercely rival sects, each claiming to possess the exclusive truth, so, too, did international Marxism. The disputes within the Communist movement were often as fierce as the conflict between Communism and its political enemies. It is in that context that Sino-Soviet relations after 1949 are best understood. There is the further consideration that as well as being Communist systems China and the USSR were also great nations, each with an extraordinary history. It is sometimes difficult to judge which was the deeper cause of their conflict - their ideological rivalry as Communist states or their mutual jealousy as great powers.

Yet in 1949 all the signs were that the PRC and the USSR would develop a close partnership. One of Mao Zedong's first statements after taking power was to declare that Communist China would 'lean to one side' in its foreign policy, that side being the Soviet Union. This was not a surprising commitment. It was to be expected that the ideo- logical affinities between the USSR and China would draw them together in a great Communist alliance. This, indeed, was the grim prospect that the USA and its allies now contemplated - a Communist monolith, containing two of the world's largest nations and stretching across two continents from central Europe to the Pacific. The USA believed that under the direction of Stalin and the Soviet Union 'half the world had gone red'.

After 1945 the USA's attitude towards other counties was largely shaped by Cold War considerations. That Mao and his followers were Communists was sufficient to frighten America into believing that the new Chinese regime was in league with the USSR. It was only later that the profound differences between Soviet and Chinese Communism were appreciated by Western observers. In the strained atmosphere of the Cold War, the American State Department assumed that Mao's objectives were the same as Stalin's. Indeed, for a time that seemed to be a realistic perception since Mao initially did acknowledge the leadership of the Soviet Union in the international revolutionary movement. The reaction of the Western world was understandable but mistaken. The creation of the Chinese People's Republic owed nothing to Stalin, and the USSR and the PRC never represented a united Communist bloc. Fundamental disagreements between the Soviet Union and Red China were present from the beginning. They were sometimes submerged but they were never far below the surface. After 1949 there were occasional periods of apparent harmony when the two Communist powers seemed to present a solid front towards the West, but the prevailing relationship was one of suspicion which at times degenerated into warlike hostility.

There were some Western sceptics who refused to accept that there was a split between the Soviet Union and Red China. They held that it was a myth, deliberately cultivated by the two powers concerned in order to deceive the West into thinking it was facing a divided enemy, whereas in reality the Sino-Soviet bloc remained a deadly anti-capitalist alliance. It is now clear that such Western scepticism was mistaken; the division in the Communist camp was a very real one.

2 The Roots of Sino-Soviet Rivalry

The reasons for the estrangement between the PRC and the USSR are many and go back well before 1949. The 4,500 mile border between China and Russia had made the two neighbours very wary of each other in tsarist times. The Bolshevik Revolution in 1917 did nothing to alter this. Lenin proudly asserted in 1918 that his new government was abandoning all claims to former tsarist territories outside Russia. Yet a year later the Bolsheviks seized Outer Mongolia, a province which the Chinese had traditionally regarded as their own. At the end of the Pacific war in 1945, Manchuria, which had been occupied by the Japanese, was returned to China but only after the withdrawing Soviet forces had stripped the region of its industrial resources, depriving China of over $2 billion worth of plant and machinery.

Even after the PRC had been established in 1949, border disputes continued to sour Sino-Soviet relations.

This long-standing national rivalry was intensified by the personal disputes that developed between the Soviet and Chinese leaders. Differences over the meaning of Marxism and how it should be applied in China had bedevilled relations between Mao and Stalin since the 1920s. Stalin had been unwilling to accept that a peasant-based movement such as Mao was leading could be genuinely revolutionary. The Marxist rules of class war dictated that true proletarian revolution had to be urban-based. Although Stalin was quite prepared to ignore Marxist dialectics when they did not fit the Soviet situation, he was rigidly dogmatic when applying them outside the USSR.

If the young Chinese Communist Party had followed the instructions it received from Stalin during the 1920s and 1930s it would have been destroyed. Stalin never fully understood the Chinese situation; he overestimated the strength of the Nationalists and underrated that of the CCP. Refusing to believe that the Chinese Communists could survive on their own, he had urged them to ally themselves with the Nationalists. He maintained this line even after it became obvious that Chiang Kaishek's principal aim was to wipe out the CCP. Even in the late 1940s, when the victory of the PLA was imminent, Stalin continued to appeal to Mao to reach a compromise with Chiang and the GMD. Stalin's insistence on this point convinced Mao that what the Soviet leader wanted was a disunited and divided China which would leave the USSR as the dominant force in Asia. This was why Mao found it hard to accept the USSR, despite its revolutionary credentials, as the true voice of international Marxism. He came increasingly to believe that what motivated the Soviet Union was crude national self-interest. He later reflected:

1   In 1945 Stalin refused China permission to carry out a revolution and
    he told us: 'Do not have a civil war. Collaborate with Chiang Kai-shek.
    Otherwise the Republic of China will collapse'. However, we did not
    obey him and the revolution succeeded. Even after the success of the
5   revolution, Stalin feared that China might degenerate into another
    Yugoslavia and that I might become another Tito [the Communist leader
    of Yugoslavia who defied Stalin]. I later went to Moscow [in 1950] and
    concluded the Sino-Soviet Treaty of Alliance. This was the result of a
    struggle. Stalin did not wish to sign the treaty; he finally signed it after
10 two months of negotiations.

The treaty to which Mao referred was the first formal agreement between Red China and the USSR. Despite Stalin's earlier doubts about the ability of the CCP to survive, the establishment of the PRC in 1949 was warmly welcomed by the Soviet Union. The Kremlin expected that this newly-formed Marxist state, vulnerable in a capitalist world, would look to the USSR, the first great Communist nation, for leadership and protection. Indeed, the US State

Department referred to the Sino-Soviet alliance as 'Moscow making puppets out of the Chinese'. However, events were to show that Mao Zedong and China were far from regarding themselves as mere creatures of Stalin and the USSR.

3 Mao and Stalin

Mao's official visit to the USSR in 1950 confirmed his doubts concerning Stalin's attitude. It is true that the Treaty, which was the first objective of his journey, provided China with its most immediate material needs, but Mao was offended by the superior air adopted by the Russians and by Stalin's deliberately offhand treatment of his Chinese guests. Mao complained that he had been dumped in a poor-quality villa outside Moscow with a rickety table-tennis table as the sole means of recreation. His hosts had made no arrangements to entertain him beyond the formal round of official meetings and banquets. His only other invitation was to the Bolshoi Theatre. Mao, whose first visit abroad this was, felt slighted. His Chinese sense of the fitness of things had been affronted. Biographers of Stalin and Mao agree in suggesting that the two leaders disliked each other as people and that this may explain why Stalin was loath to meet Mao except formally. Their personalities tended to conflict. Arguably, this was because they were so similar in type. But, whatever the psychological explanation, the outcome was that relations between the two great Communist powers were severely strained by the animus that developed between their leaders.

It soon became apparent that Mao and the Chinese had good reason for distrusting Stalin. They realised soon after the 1950 Treaty had been signed that the Soviet Union was intent on exploiting the

Mao (far left)   *Stalin (centre)*   *Khrushchev (far right)*
The leaders of the USSR and the PRC in Moscow, 1950

agreement in its own favour. This was in spite of Mao's initial belief that the hard-won Treaty had obligated the USSR to provide China with expertise and aid at low cost. Its wording had appeared to promise much:

1 Each Contracting Party undertakes, in a spirit of friendship and co-operation and in conformity with the principles of equality, mutual benefit
   and mutual respect for the national sovereignty and territorial integrity
   and non-interference in the internal affairs of the other Contracting
5 Party, to develop and consolidate economic and cultural ties between
   China and the Soviet Union, to render the other all possible economic
   assistance.

But Stalin had struck a hard bargain. Under the 1950 treaty Soviet aid was to be advanced as a loan not a gift; the PRC had to undertake to repay the full amount plus interest (see page 26). Nikita Khrushchev, a later Soviet leader, admitted that the Treaty had betrayed China: 'It was an insult to the Chinese people. For centuries the French, English and Americans had been exploiting China, and now the Soviet Union was moving in'. Mao's recognition that China had been ill used put the young Sino-Soviet partnership under great stress. The tension was felt as early as the Korean War (1950-53). Mao remarked that China had to pay 'down to the last rifle and bullet' for the Soviet materiel it received during that conflict. There were also suggestions that Stalin deliberately prevented an early armistice being reached in Korea in order to exhaust the Chinese. It was certainly the case that almost immediately after Stalin's death in 1953 a truce was negotiated.

Why did Mao, in spite of his deep reservations about Stalin's motives, allow Soviet influence to impose itself on China? The influence was not simply ideological. The Soviet planners and engineers who came to the PRC in its early years left a heavy imprint on China's physical appearance. Over two hundred construction projects were undertaken by the USSR in China during the 1950s. New public buildings and squares bore the Soviet stamp. In Beijing many of China's most delicate and antique structures were razed to be replaced by Soviet-style functional eyesores, which most Chinese loathed as an aesthetic affront. But, as Mao saw it, this was the price that had to be paid for the material aid that China needed from the USSR. Soviet scientific techniques were also given priority in China. Even when these, in contrast to Western advances, were dated and cumbersome they were deemed to be superior since they represented 'socialist science'. One tragic example of the folly was the disastrous effect of China's commitment to the pseudo-science of Lysenkoism during the Great Leap Forward of the late 1950s (see page 29). The USSR's military assistance was also judged to be necessary, at least for the time being. The hard fact was that China's international isolation meant that it could not easily obtain resources and expertise from other than the Soviet Union. This remained the position until the

1960s when China was able to mount its own independent nuclear-research programme.

4 China and De-Stalinisation

Since it had principally been Stalin's uncompromising manner that had caused tension between Moscow and Beijing, it was reasonable to expect that after the Soviet leader's death in 1953 relations would ease. This appeared to happen at first; something of a Sino-Soviet 'honeymoon' period intervened in the mid 1950s. The new Soviet leaders were willing to provide China with further loans and technology. But even as better relations developed, events undermined the possibility of a genuine partnership. A key event was the 'secret speech' delivered in Moscow in October 1956 by Nikita Khrushchev, who had emerged from the power struggle that followed Stalin's death as the leading figure in the Soviet Union. Khrushchev staggered the USSR and the Communist world by launching a detailed attack on Stalin for his 'crimes against the Party'. A particular charge that had obvious resonance in China was that Stalin had engaged in a 'cult of personality', a reference to the enormous power that he had taken into his own hands at the expense of the Party.

While Mao had had profound differences with Stalin, he was deeply disturbed by the ferocity of this assault upon Stalin's reputation. He read the denunciation of the cult of personality as a calculated criticism of his own style of leadership in China. Mao was also disturbed by the political developments that occurred in Eastern Europe in the wake of the de-Stalinisation programme. Greater freedom appeared to be offered to the Soviet satellites to criticise their Communist governments and to question their subordination to the USSR. This had not been Khrushchev's intention, as he was quick to demonstrate by ordering the suppression of the anti-Soviet rising in Hungary in November 1956. But for Mao the Hungarian rising and those that had occurred in Poland and East Germany were the direct result of the failure of the Soviet Union's post-Stalin leadership to control the forces of reaction within the Communist bloc.

He was equally offended by the softening of the Soviet attitude towards the West. Moscow now seemed to accept that there were alternative ways of achieving revolution in the modern world other than by armed struggle. Khrushchev had by the late 1950s concluded that in a world of nuclear superpowers the Marxist-Leninist notion of a final violent conflict between the international proletariat and the forces of capitalism was no longer acceptable. He said that had comrade Lenin lived in a nuclear age he would have modified the rigidity of his original contention. Mao condemned this adjustment as heresy. He believed that the final struggle was unavoidable and that it was the duty of all revolutionaries not only to prepare for it but also to hasten its coming. For Mao, Khrushchev's policy of de-Stalinisation was clear evidence that Soviet Communism had taken the wrong path.

Disturbed by the murmurings in the Marxist camp, Khrushchev in 1957 convened a conference in Moscow of the world's Communist parties. His broad aim was to repair the differences between the USSR and the other Marxist countries. His particular hope was that he could lay Stalin's ghost by bringing Tito and Yugoslavia back into the Soviet fold. However, at the last moment Tito declined to attend. This disappointed Mao whose own reluctance to visit the Soviet Union at Moscow's bidding had been overcome only by the thought that Tito would be there. Nevertheless, since the arrangements were too advanced to cancel, Mao did attend. This was the second and last time he travelled outside China. At the meeting he was still prepared to recognise the USSR's unique place in the history of proletarian revolution. He also approved a Sino-Soviet declaration which expressed China's readiness to co-operate. But at the same time Mao let it be known that he regarded Moscow's approach to the West as too accommodating. He called on the Soviet Union to abandon 'revisionism', the term that Communist hard-liners used to denounce any straying from what they regarded as orthodox Marxism-Leninism. Rather than making concessions to capitalism, it was the Soviet Union's revolutionary duty to fight the class war by fully supporting the liberation movements worldwide. This could not be done by extending peaceful overtures to class enemies - the imperialist Western nations. What underlay Mao's words was his suspicion that the Soviet Union was following a policy of detente with the West in order to leave China internationally isolated.

Mao's chief spokesman at the Moscow meeting was Deng Xiaoping, who excelled himself in expounding the Chinese version of international revolution. Deng argued powerfully that the proletarian world revolution was achievable only through armed struggle; capitalism had to be overcome by force. In a tense series of exchanges he got the better of the leading Soviet political theorist, Mikhail Suslov, and won the admiration, if not the open support, of many of the other delegates. The Russian hosts were embarrassed and angered by Deng's performance.

5 Mao and Khrushchev

Despite the Chinese challenge to the Soviet Union's ideological primacy, Khrushchev persisted in his attempt to improve the USSR's relations with the PRC. In 1958, following the mishandling by Pavel Yudin, the Soviet Ambassador in China, of negotiations regarding a joint Sino-Soviet naval programme, Khrushchev flew to Beijing to meet Mao again. His main purpose was to assure Mao that Yudin had given the wrong impression by suggesting that China's navy must be brought under Soviet control. Mao, however, was disinclined to listen. In a tit-for-tat for the poor treatment he had endured during his visits to Moscow, Mao deliberately set out to make Khrushchev uncomfortable. He arranged for the Soviet delegation to be put up at a hotel without air-conditioning; the Russians sweltered in Beijing's fierce summer heat and were plagued by mosquitoes. In one notorious incident Mao insisted that a round of talks take place in his private pool. Mao was a regular swimmer; Khrushchev hated the water. Nonetheless, to humour his host Khrushchev agreed. In a pair of baggy shorts and squeezed into a barely-buoyant rubber ring, the rotund Soviet leader desperately floundered and splashed while interpreters raced round the pool's edge trying to make sense of his gurgled replies to Mao's questions. The talks were not a success.

Their failure was not simply the result of the swimming-pool farce. Deng Xiaoping was again let loose to savage the Russian delegation as he had in Moscow. He attacked the USSR for its 'great nation, great party chauvinism', in believing that it was the only true interpreter of Marxist-Leninism. Deng repeated Mao's accusation that the technical advisers sent to China by Moscow were in fact Soviet spies. He charged the Soviet Union with betraying the international Communist movement. It is often suggested that it was Mao's remembrance of Deng Xiaoping's brilliant exposition of Maoist revolutionary theory at these two meetings that saved Deng from harsher treatment at the time of his disgrace in the Cultural Revolution in 1966 (see page 42).

In 1958 the simmering Taiwan issue provided another test of the genuineness of Sino-Soviet sympathies. Without consulting Moscow, Mao ordered a build-up of troop movements in the region which seemed to be a preparation for a full-scale assault on the Nationalist-held island. The United States responded by preparing for war with mainland China (see page 94). In the event, Mao held back from a direct attack on Taiwan. One of the reasons he gave was that the USSR had declined to give China even moral support. Khrushchev's countered by saying that he was not willing to put the USSR at risk by 'testing the stability of the capitalist system'. He denounced Mao and the Chinese as 'Trotskyists'; they were so concerned with the notion of world revolution that they had lost all sense of political reality. The resulting deterioration in relations led the Soviet Union to withdraw its economic advisers from China and to cancel its commercial contracts there.

The steep decline in Sino-Soviet understanding was not halted by Moscow's reaction to China's Great Leap Forward. In 1959 Mao was enraged by the news that the Soviet Union had dismissed his attempt to revolutionise the Chinese economy as faulty in design and bungled in practice. He was particularly angered by rumours that one of his own chiefs-of-staff, Marshal Peng Dehuai, had passed on information to Moscow regarding the widespread starvation that the Great Leap had caused (see page 32).

In retaliation for what Mao saw as the Soviet Union's attempt to undermine China's standing among the Communist nations, the PRC gave support to those countries which defied the USSR. China had strongly criticised de-Stalinisation for the encouragement it had given to reaction and counter-revolution in the Eastern-bloc countries. Yet, when the Chinese leaders saw the chance to embarrass the Soviet Union by supporting the socialist countries hostile to the USSR, they took it. Albania was a clear example. In 1961, following the Soviet Union's withdrawal of its aid to Albania, the PRC stepped in to supply it with money and technical assistance. It did not matter that Albania was run by an oppressive neo-Stalinist regime and was a minor player on the socialist stage. It was enough for the Chinese that it was on bad terms with the USSR.

It was the Albanian question that brought matters to a head and led to the severing of diplomatic relations between the Soviet Union and the PRC. The occasion was Zhou Enlai's walk-out from the 1961 Moscow Congress of the Communist Party of the Soviet Union (CPSU), to which China had been invited as an observer. Khrushchev's speech at the Congress, abusing the Albanian Communist leaders for their backward Stalinist ways, was interpreted by the Chinese as a deliberately offensive attack upon themselves. Having expected such an onslaught Zhou and the Chinese delegation quit the hall in accordance with a rehearsed plan. This dramatic gesture was the climax to a decade of Sino-Soviet recrimination. Nearly twenty-five years were to elapse before the two Communist powers achieved a rapprochement.

The collapse of diplomatic relations encouraged the Soviet and Chinese leaders to be still more caustic in their personal references to each other. Khrushchev abused Mao as an 'Asian Hitler' and 'a living corpse'. Mao countered by dismissing his Russian adversary as 'a redundant old boot'. Such exchanges of insults at the highest level had the effect of sharpening the border disputes between the USSR and China. Throughout the 1960s and 1970s local confrontations were frequent and often violent. During this period, the USSR committed nearly fifty Red Army divisions to defend its Asian frontiers. China angrily asserted that the refusal of the USSR to return the Chinese territories that Russia had acquired by the 'unequal treaties' of the nineteenth century made it as guilty of imperialism as the original tsarist expropriators. Beijing's news agency spoke of the 'anti-Chinese atrocities of the new tsars'. The Chinese were especially incensed by the USSR's attitude during the Sino-Indian war that broke out on the Tibetan border in 1962 (see page 107). The Soviet Union was formally neutral but it provided India with MIG fighters and its moral support was all on India's side. Mao viewed the offer by Kosygin, the USSR's foreign minister, to act as mediator between the PRC and India as hypocrisy. He rejected it as a yet another attempt by the Soviet Union to undermine China's international standing.

An even more dramatic international development in 1962 provided China with the opportunity to ridicule the Soviet Union's claim to the leadership of world revolution. In that year the USSR exploited its influence over Fidel Castro's Communist Cuba to install rockets and nuclear warheads on the island. Since Cuba stood only ninety miles off the coast of the USA, President Kennedy demanded the withdrawal of the weapons. After a tense stand-off Khrushchev complied. China scorned Moscow for its original 'adventurism' in siting detectable nuclear warheads in Cuba and for its subsequent 'capitulationism' in abjectly bowing to the American threat to retaliate. Was this, China asked contemptuously, the way to inspire the world's struggling masses in their fight against American imperialism?

6 Conflicting Concepts of Revolution

a) The Issue of Coexistence

The broad response in the West to the ending of the Cuban missile crisis was to congratulate both Kennedy and Khrushchev for their statesmanship in stepping back from the brink and reaching a compromise, which involved the Soviet missiles being withdrawn from Cuba and American bases being closed in Turkey. While Kennedy was accorded the greater share of credit, many influential commentators paid tribute to Khrushchev's sense of responsibility in accepting that war between great nations was no longer a genuine option in the nuclear age. Khrushchev's behaviour in resolving the crisis was interpreted as an extension of his policy of coexistence with the West, and therefore as being highly laudable. This was not how the Chinese saw it. For them coexistence was a betrayal of the revolution. Instead of achieving peace, the policy simply played into the hands of the imperialist powers by settling issues on their terms. Genuine coexistence could occur only between equal nations. But in Marxist dialectics all pre-revolutionary states were unequal since they were in subjection to the exploiting capitalist powers. In a formal statement in 1963 the CCP explained the fallacy of coexistence and why China would not engage in it:

1   Only after victory in the revolution is it possible and necessary for the proletariat to pursue the policy of peaceful coexistence. As for oppressed peoples and nations, their task is to strive for their own liberation and overthrow the rule of imperialism and its lackeys. They should
5   not practise peaceful coexistence with the imperialists and their lackeys, nor is it possible for them to do so. It is therefore wrong to apply peaceful coexistence to the relations between oppressed and oppressor classes and between oppressed and oppressor nations, or to stretch the socialist countries' policy of peaceful coexistence so as to make it the
10 policy of the Communist Parties and the revolutionary people in the capitalist world, or to subordinate the revolutionary struggles of the oppressed peoples and nations to it.

The Soviet response was to accuse the Chinese of total irresponsibility. It was arrogant and dangerous of China to claim to speak for the international working class:

1 We might ask the Chinese comrades, who offer to build a beautiful future on the ruins of the old world destroyed by thermo-nuclear war: did they consult, on this issue, the working class of countries where imperialism is in power? The working class of the capitalist
5 countries would be sure to tell them: are we asking you to unleash war and destroy our countries in the process of destroying the imperialists? The working class, the working people, will ask such 'revolutionaries':What right have you to decide for us questions involving our very existence and our class struggle - we too want socialism, but we
10 want to win it through the class struggle, not by unleashing a world thermo-nuclear war.

At the time of his fall from power in the USSR in 1964, Khrushchev was still trying to convince the rest of the Marxist world that the Maoist brand of Communism was heretical. His policy of isolating China was continued by the collective leadership that superseded him. In the fierce Sino-Soviet propaganda war each side accused the other of a long list of crimes against Communism. The USSR resurrected the spectre of the 'yellow peril', arguing that China was prepared to use its vast population to swamp the West, beginning with the USSR. Mao and his colleagues were branded as 'petty bourgeois', no longer true Communists. The Cultural Revolution that began in 1966 was cited as an example of China's raging fanaticism, a fanaticism which threatened to destroy the world. For good measure, the Soviet Union alleged that the PRC was trading illicitly with apartheid South Africa, receiving assistance from West Germany in its nuclear research, developing a worldwide opium trade, and secretly sending supplies to the American forces in Vietnam.

b) Mao's Concept of Continuing Revolution

Mao Zedong responded to the Soviet insults by describing the USSR's leaders as 'social fascists' who were perverting Marxism. He condemned their reforms of the Soviet economy as a return to capitalism and their moves towards coexistence as collusion with the imperialist West. Mao called on Communists in all other countries to reject the USSR's lead and develop their own form of true Marxism along Chinese lines. The vital concept for Mao was that of 'continuing revolution'. Fierce ideological battles over this notion had been fought earlier within the Soviet Union. Trotsky, Stalin's arch opponent in the 1920s and 1930s, had made 'continuing' or 'permanent' revolution the essence of Marxism-Leninism. For Trotsky revolution was not an event but a process whose continuity was the guarantee of the ultimate triumph of the international proletariat. Revolutions which regarded themselves as complete or which were confined to individual countries would cease to be revolutions and would fall prey to reaction. Mao's own definition corresponded to Trotsky's:

1 Continuing revolution. Our revolutions come one after another. Starting from the seizure of power in the whole country in 1949, there followed in quick succession the anti-feudal land reform, the agricultural co-oper-ativization, and the socialist reconstruction of private industries,
5 commerce, and handicrafts ... Now we must start a technological revo-lution so that we may overtake Britain in fifteen or more years ... After fifteen years, when our foodstuffs and iron and steel become plentiful, we shall take a much greater initiative. Our revolutions are like battles. After a victory, we must at once put forward a new task. In this way,
10 cadres and the masses will forever be filled with revolutionary fervour.

The Sino-Soviet quarrel over the meaning of revolution raised the demanding question as to which nation was the real leader of the Communist world. Was it the USSR, direct heir of the great 1917 Revolution, or China, whose peasant-based revolution in 1949 offered a model and inspiration for all oppressed peoples. In strict Marxist theory, true proletarian revolution could occur only in an urban, industrial society. According to the Kremlin's theoreticians, China as a preponderantly peasant society could not be a fully developed Communist state. They asserted that Mao had distorted Marxism to make it fit the Chinese context. The CCP's ideologists reacted angrily to the dismissal of Maoism as an inferior Marxist model. They retali-ated by accusing the Soviet Union of betraying the cause of world revolution by attempting to lead the Communist states into a suicidal policy of detente with the West.

c) The Nuclear Issue

The dispute between the Soviet Union and China over the question of coexistence with the West was at its fiercest in their disagreement over the Test Ban Treaty of 1963. Under the Treaty, the USSR and the Western nuclear powers jointly pledged themselves to end the atmos-pheric testing of atomic weapons. Mao viewed the Treaty as another step by the Soviet Union towards the abandonment of its revolu-tionary role. Instead of confronting imperialism, the USSR was co-operating with it: 'Soviet revisionist collaborators are uniting with the running dogs of capitalism'. Khrushchev's rejoinder was that rather than seek peace the Chinese wished to see East and West destroy themselves in nuclear war leaving China free to dominate what was left of the world. What gave particular irony to Khrushchev's charge was that China was only a year away from exploding its own atomic bomb.

Since the 1950s Mao Zedong had been infuriated by the attitude of Stalin and successive Soviet leaders over the nuclear question.

Moscow's stance was that if China wanted Soviet assistance in its nuclear programme it must give the USSR a controlling hand in the PRC's defence policy. This was too much for Mao. The Soviet demand confirmed his judgement that the USSR was not a genuine partner in the cause of international socialism. It redoubled his determination to make China a superpower by achieving nuclear status unaided. Refusing to be deterred by the withdrawal of Soviet scientists in 1960, China pressed on with its own research programme. Its commitment was illustrated by the painstaking piecing together by the PRC's scientists of the records that the Soviet advisers had shredded before their hurried departure. Such efforts reaped their reward. In 1964 Communist China detonated its first atomic device and three years later its first hydrogen bomb. It was now in a position to face the world on equal terms with the other nuclear powers. This remarkable achievement allowed the PRC to mock the USSR's refusal to assist. The first Chinese bomb was codenamed 59/6 a reference to the year and month in which the Soviet technicians had withdrawn from China. Mao recorded gloatingly:

1   Modern weapons, guided missiles, and atom bombs were made very quickly, and we produced a hydrogen bomb in only two years and eight months. Our development has been faster than that of America, Britain and France. We are now in fourth place in the world. Guided missiles
5   and atom bombs are great achievements. This is the result of Khrushchev's 'help'. By withdrawing the experts he forced us to take our own road. We should give him a big medal.

China's emergence as a superpower had profound ramifications. Unlike the West and the Soviet Union, China seemed not to have the same awesome fear of nuclear war. Mao's attitude and utterances seemed to suggest that he was willing to consider the use of atomic weapons as a logical progression in diplomacy. An earlier CCP statement had revealed that China calculated it could survive a nuclear war:

1   On the debris of a dead imperialism, the victorious [Chinese] people would create very swiftly a civilisation thousands of times higher than the capitalist system and a truly beautiful future for themselves. The conclusion can only be this: whichever way you look at it, none of the
5   new techniques like atomic energy, rocketry and so on has changed, as alleged by modern revisionists, the basic characteristics of the epoch of imperialism and proletarian revolution pointed out by Lenin.

It was significant that when the massive earthquake occurred at Tangshan in 1976 it was looked upon by the Chinese as a test run for a nuclear disaster (see page 54). Displaying the traditional Chinese sense of practicality, the authorities saw it as a means of measuring their readiness to deal with the after effects of a nuclear explosion. Mao believed that China's development of a hydrogen bomb was of more than military significance. As a superpower that could no longer be ignored or bullied in international affairs, China now stood as the true champion of the oppressed nations of the world:

> 1 The success of China's hydrogen bomb test has further broken the nuclear monopoly of United States imperialism and Soviet revisionism and dealt a telling blow at their policy of nuclear blackmail. It is a very great encouragement and support to the Vietnamese people in their
> 5 heroic war against United States' aggression and for national salvation, to the Arab people in their resistance to aggression by the United States and British imperialists and their tool, Israel, and to the revolutionary people of the whole world.

7 The PRC and Brezhnev

The emergence by the late 1960s of Leonid Brezhnev as leader of the USSR did nothing to improve Sino-Soviet relations. Brezhnev, who was to remain at the Soviet helm until 1982, was a Stalinist in foreign policy. His demand, often referred to as the 'Brezhnev doctrine', was that in order to maintain socialist solidarity all the Eastern bloc states accept and follow the leadership of the Soviet Union. If any of them should fail in this they were to be disciplined by the other states acting as 'a socialist community' under the direction of the USSR. The doctrine was put into practice in the crushing of 'the Prague spring' in 1968; Soviet tanks rolled into the Czechoslovak capital to suppress the Communist government, which under Alexander Dubcek had attempted to assert its independence of Soviet control. While Mao had no time for counter-revolution in Communist states he was unwilling to accept the right of the USSR, which by his reckoning was no longer truly socialist, to impose its authority on the members of the Marxist camp.

At Brezhnev's prompting, a third international Communist conference was convened in Moscow in 1969 with the aim of outlawing China. However, the Soviet invasion of Czechoslovakia in the previous year had weakened the USSR's moral authority and the conference failed to produce a clear plan of action. The fact was that international Communism had seriously fragmented. 1969 marked perhaps the lowest point in the relations of the two Communist superpowers. Serious border incidents threatened to turn into full-scale war. Mao began to regret that in constructing the Third Line its position had been dictated by fear of American attack; its siting close to the Soviet border made it vulnerable to the new enemy - the USSR. In an extraordinary development the PRC and the Soviet reorientated their nuclear-armed rockets so that they now faced inwards towards each other rather than outwards towards their Western enemies. This may have been bluff and counter-bluff but there was no doubting that Sino-Soviet relations had reached their nadir. This was powerfully expressed in Lin Biao's denunciation of Brezhnev and the Soviet 'revisionists':

1 Since Brezhnev came to power, with its baton becoming less and less effective and its difficulties at home and abroad growing more and more serious, the Soviet revisionist renegade clique has been practising social imperialism and social fascism more frantically than ever. In order to
5 justify its aggression and plunder, the Soviet revisionist renegade Clique trumpets the so-called theory of 'limited sovereignty', the theory of 'international dictatorship' and the theory of 'socialist community'. What does all this stuff mean? It means that your sovereignty is 'limited', while his is unlimited ... He will exercise 'international dictatorship' over you
10 - dictatorship over the people of other countries, in order to form the 'socialist community' ruled by the new czar, that is, colonies of social imperialism, just like the 'new order of Europe' of Hitler, the 'Great East Asia Co-Prosperity Sphere' of Japanese militarism and the 'free world community' of the United States.

8 Sino-Soviet Rivalry in Indochina

Indochina, made up principally of Laos, Cambodia and Vietnam, was a vitally strategic area on China's southern border. As early as the 1950s Communist China had been diplomatically involved in the region. In 1954 the PRC was officially present at the Geneva Conference, which met to draw up the peace terms following the defeat of France, the dominant colonial power in the area. The French had been overcome by a set of national resistance movements (the Vietminh) in which the Communists of north Vietnam, led by Ho Chi Minh, had taken the most prominent part. Zhou Enlai played an important role at the Geneva talks, this despite being publicly snubbed by John Foster Dulles, the American Secretary of State, who objected to the presence of representatives of Red China. Zhou helped steer the often-acrimonious discussions towards a compromise settlement. The main parties - France, the United States, the USSR and the Vietnamese - eventually agreed on a number of key resolutions. France totally withdrew from the region. Laos and Cambodia were recognised as independent states, while Vietnam was divided along the 17th parallel between a Communist-dominated North and a non-Communist South. The partition was intended to be only temporary; elections were to be held within two years to select a government for a united Vietnam. However, the Americans, fearful that if elections were held Ho's Vietminh would win, refused to accept that part of the Geneva settlement. This led the USA subsequently into supporting a series of corrupt and inefficient south Vietnamese regimes simply on the grounds that they were anti-Communist. Ho Chi Minh's response was to urge the nationalists in the south to join the Vietminh. In 1960 a National Liberation Front (NLF) was set up in the south by Ho's supporters with the aim of uniting both parts of Vietnam under Communist rule. The NLF's troops were known as the Viet Cong.

This was the prelude to a long civil war in Vietnam into which the United States was increasingly drawn. Between 1963 and its eventual humiliating withdrawal in 1975, the USA tried unavailingly, and at a huge cost in men and resources, to overcome the Viet Cong and establish a stable anti-Communist south Vietnam. But in 1975 the Viet Cong finally overran the south; a year later a single Socialist Republic of Vietnam was created. Mao's China was not directly involved in the Vietnam War, but it gave moral and diplomatic support to Ho Chi Minh. The PRC kept up a running condemnation of 'naked American imperialism'. It also continued the programme it had begun during the Vietminh war against the French of supplying Ho's forces with arms and equipment.

Yet Red China was not to reap the benefits of its assistance to the Vietnamese Communists. The reason was that the USSR had stolen a march on the PRC. Moscow, believing that if it could intrude success-fully into south-east Asia it would gain an additional victory in its ideo-logical struggle with China, had throughout the Vietnam war of 1963-75 kept the North Vietnamese supplied with aid and arms. Soviet influence increased still further after the Americans withdrew from Vietnam in 1975 and the whole country came under Communist control. The USSR now openly adopted Vietnam as its protege and in 1978 concluded a 'Soviet-Vietnamese Treaty of Peace and Friendship'.

China's realisation that it had lost out to the USSR over Vietnam led it to seek compensation by developing close ties with Cambodia (Kampuchea), Vietnam's western neighbour. Cambodia, like Vietnam had also undergone a recent Marxist revolution. In 1975 Pol Pot, the leader of the Cambodian Communists (the Khmer Rouge), had seized power after a successful guerilla war modelled on Maoist strategy. The savagery of Pol Pot's regime (1975-79) in crushing oppo-sition outstripped even the excesses of China's Cultural Revolution. It was estimated that nearly two and a half million out of Cambodia's population of seven million were killed in this brief period. However, Pol Pot's Maoist credentials made him a hero to the Chinese. When, following a border dispute in 1978 between the two newly-Communist neighbours, the Vietnamese launched a major offensive into Cambodia to overthrow Pol Pot, Communist China immediately came to his aid by a reverse invasion of Vietnam. Both sides, the Soviet-backed Vietnamese and the PRC-supported Cambodians, claimed that the other had made the first aggressive move. The exact truth is unclear but what is not in doubt is that the Vietnamese won the ensuing conflict. The official PRC version of events led the Chinese people to believe that the PLA had gained a resounding military success. This was the precise opposite of what had happened. The PLA had suffered heavy casualties and had been forced to withdraw from Vietnam, having failed to prevent Pol Pot's overthrow by the Vietnamese. Although it was withheld from public knowledge in

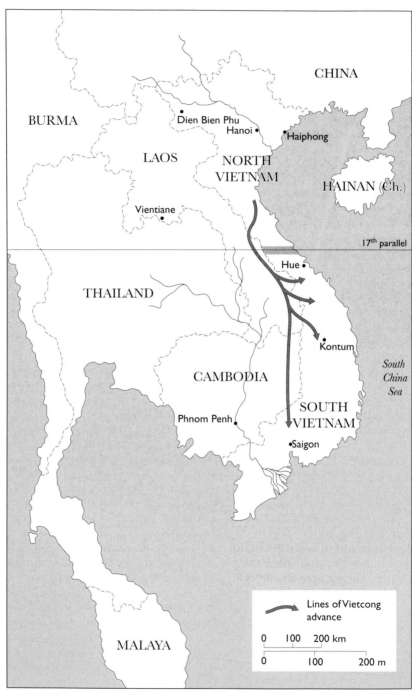

A map of Indochina

China, the PRC had undergone a major set-back in its propaganda war with the USSR for the leadership of international Marxism.

9 The End of Sino-Soviet Rivalry

Mao's death in 1976, which was soon followed by the overthrow of the fanatically anti-Soviet Gang of Four, greatly eased Sino-Soviet relations. Despite the difficulties over Vietnam, the new leaders of the PRC, Deng Xiaoping in particular, adopted a much more tolerant line towards both the USSR and the West. Deng Xiaoping may be said to have adopted Zhou Enlai's accommodating style as an international statesman. He deliberately toned down the aggressive anti-Soviet approach which he had shown while serving under Mao. The possibility of nuclear war between China and either the USA or the USSR became increasingly remote. Although full diplomatic relations between Moscow and Beijing were not restored, the death of the uncompromising Brezhnev in 1982 did much to soften the former tensions.

The rise of Mikhail Gorbachev to the leadership of the USSR in 1985 further reduced the hardness of Soviet attitudes towards the world at large and China in particular. Although a product of the same Stalinist political system that had produced Khrushchev and Brezhnev, Gorbachev was much less rigid in his thinking and much more attractive in personal style. Since Deng Xiaoping was already following the most tolerant line yet adopted by the PRC in its foreign relations, there were strong grounds for anticipating that he and Gorbachev would take steps to end a generation of Sino-Soviet bitterness. However, there was a particular difficulty to be overcome - the Soviet occupation of Afghanistan. This had begun under Brezhnev in 1979 and had been continually condemned by the PRC. Beijing viewed it not as a legitimate guarding by the Soviet Union of its vulnerable boundaries but as part of its aggressive strategy of massing large numbers of troops on China's borders.

The problem was not immediately resolved but there was certainly a relaxing of tension between Moscow and Beijing. By 1986 new trade agreements had been drafted and procedures had begun for the restoration of full diplomatic relations. Such was the lessening of the old enmities that when the USSR did eventually begin its withdrawal from Afghanistan in 1989 Gorbachev was invited to pay an official visit to Beijing in that same year. However, what should have been a historic event, the first personal contact between Chinese and Soviet leaders for over twenty years, was overshadowed by the dramatic developments within China. Gorbachev's arrival in Beijing coincided with the bloody climax of the pro-democracy demonstration (see page 79). A particular embarrassment for the PRC leaders was that the pro-democracy activists welcomed Gorbachev as a reforming progressive whose policies of 'glasnost' (open government) and 'perestroika' (restructuring) had introduced into the Soviet Union the very changes that reformers were urging in China.

In the event Gorbachev's popularity with the democrats in China did not long embarrass the Chinese leaders for the simple reason that Gorbachev was soon to be one of the victims of his own reforms. The wholesale collapse of Communism in eastern Europe between 1988 and 1991 included the abandonment by the CPSU in 1990 of its 'leading role', followed a year later by the dissolution of the USSR. The end of the Soviet Union necessarily meant the end of Sino-Soviet rivalry for the leadership of the Marxist world. Since Soviet Communism could no longer impose itself on its own nation it was scarcely in a position to compete with the Chinese form.

The pertinent question now was what remained of China's commitment to international revolution. The rapid withering of Communism as a world force left the PRC isolated in the 1990s as the only major nation that officially still espoused Marxism as its guiding creed. Just how deeply the Chinese government believed in Communism at this late stage is questionable. Lip service continued to be paid to the concept of international revolution, but it was difficult to believe that the Chinese leaders, having witnessed the collapse of the USSR, would be prepared to put their own position at risk by pursuing some highly dangerous global objective. Their essential aim was to ensure their own political survival by consolidating China's position as a major nation that had embraced modernity.

Studying 'China and International Revolution'

Three critical areas can be identified in this chapter: 1. Sino-Soviet rivalry; 2. China and de-Stalinisation; 3. Conflicting concepts of revolution.

1. Sino-Soviet Rivalry

Key Question: To what extent was Sino-Soviet rivalry caused by the personal antipathy between Stalin and Mao?

Sections 1, 2 and 3 of this chapter are the required reading. It would also be helpful to study Section 2a in Chapter 1.

Points to Consider: The 'to what extent' aspect of the question invites you to place the Stalin-Mao rivalry in order of importance with the other factors that created tension between the USSR and the China. Certain points present themselves: national rivalry, the long-standing territorial disputes between Russia and China and the ideological divide between two brands of applied Marxism. Are these factors all of equal weight? You may wish to consider whether there are any significant factors that predate the creation of the PRC. This point, of course, introduces the key area of the debate. Was it the falling out of Mao and Stalin over the strategy to be followed in China that deepened the division between the Soviet Union and the Chinese revolutionaries? What Mao most resented was that Stalin had never had faith in the CCP. Even after Mao's triumph in 1949 Stalin was grudging in his admiration for the Chinese Communists. Weight should be given to this point in your answer. How important a part of the story is the 1950 Sino-Soviet treaty? It was Mao's realisation that the CCP had been exploited that confirmed his long-held belief that Stalin and the Soviet Union were no friends of the CCP. An obvious conclusion is therefore that Stalin's grudge match with Mao certainly exacerbated the rivalry between the two Communist powers. But here a qualification needs to be introduced. Looking ahead it is clear that Sino-Soviet relations became still more bitter after Stalin's death. The conflict between Mao and Khrushchev was to reach the verge of nuclear confrontation. Does this suggest that while certainly a cause of national tensions the Mao-Stalin rivalry is perhaps best viewed as belonging to a continuum of national and ideological conflict between Russia and China?

2. **China and De-Stalinisation**
   Key Question: Examine the impact of de-Stalinisation on Communist China.
   Sections 3, 4 and 5 of this chapter provide the main coverage.
   Points to Consider: A definition of de-Stalinisation is clearly called for. It would be worth your considering the way the term may be variously interpreted. Did the term have the same meaning in Mao's China as in Khrushchev's Russia? A suggested starting point is the brief 'honeymoon period' in Sino-Soviet relations which followed Stalin's death in 1953. Insofar as tensions had been caused by Stalin's uncompromising stance, it might be expected that relations would now improve. Why did this not happen? To answer this you need to explain Khrushchev's purpose in launching de-Stalinisation within the Soviet Union. It would be helpful at this point to describe the main features of de-Stalinisation as the Chinese saw them - the attack on the cult of personality, the encouragement of counter-revolution and detente with the West. In Mao's eyes, the first was an attack on his own leadership of China while the second and third were a betrayal of the cause of international revolution. Attempts to resolve Sino-Soviet differences failed and the situation rapidly deteriorated into a vicious ideological war. It would be worth your assessing how much of this was a matter of genuine principle and how much was due to personal rivalry between Mao and Khrushchev who allowed the dispute between the two Communist superpowers to degenerate into crude insults and name-calling. This farcical aspect has to be weighed against the fissures in world Marxism that de-Stalinisation had revealed.

3. Conflicting Concepts of Revolution
Key Question: Examine the significance of Mao's concept of 'continuing revolution'.

Sections 5 and 6 of this chapter provide the relevant material.

Points to Consider: An obvious starting point is to define what you understand by the key term 'continuing revolution'. Only then can you effectively consider the significance of Mao's concept. It would help if you were to explain that Mao's political ideas evolved over time and were shaped by his practical experiences as a revolutionary. He rejected dictation from Stalin as to how Marxism should be applied in China. This is where the question of significance can be addressed. If Marxism-Leninism is regarded as revolutionary orthodoxy does that make Mao a heretic? His insistence that the peasant movement he had led to victory in 1949 fulfilled the demands of genuine proletarian revolution put him at variance with Stalin's Soviet Union whose theorists dismissed Maoism as an imperfect and inferior form of Communism. It was this that lay at the heart of the Sino-Soviet conflict over the right to lead the international Marxist movement. Mao countered what he regarded as the USSR's betrayal of Communism in its de-Stalinisation programme by stressing the absolute necessity of treating revolution not as an event but as process of continual renewal and purification. This is the point where you might consider the relevance of Trotsky's notion of 'permanent revolution'. Trotsky, the Soviet outcast, had warned against established Communist governments becoming self-perpetuating bureaucracies. Is the Cultural Revolution in China best understood as a Mao's response to this warning? You may wish to develop this point into a consideration of whether Mao's continuing revolution was international rather than national in its significance. Perhaps, in unleashing the Cultural Revolution Mao was attempting not merely to rid China of 'bad elements' but to demonstrate to the world the integrity and superiority of Chinese Communism.

Source analysis - 'China and International Revolution'

The following is an analysis of a key document relating to the break down of Sino-Soviet relations in the Brezhnev years. It appears on page 126.

1 - Context
In 1969 Sino-Soviet relations reached their lowest ebb. The USSR made formal moves to outlaw the PRC from the international Communist movement and Moscow and Beijing began to prepare for war. It was in this atmosphere than Lin Biao delivered his attack upon Brezhnev and the Soviet leaders.

2 - Meaning

Lin brands the Brezhnev government as a 'revisionist renegade clique'. These were not arbitrary insults. In the language of Marxist dialectics, these words carried great power. Revisionism was the worst crime in the Marxist book; it meant abandonment of the truths of scientific Communism. The 'renegade clique' reference was meant to suggest that the Soviet Union's revolution had been usurped by a self-regarding oligarchy. Lin's condemnation expands into an attack on the Soviet leaders for attempting to impose their authority on the international revolutionary movement by establishing 'international dictatorship' over the other Marxist states and parties. The extract closes with the ultimate insult when Lin likens the plans for extending Soviet authority to the schemes drawn up by Hitler's Nazis and Japan's militarists for the domination of Europe and Asia.

3 - Significance

The bitterness which infuses Lin's onslaught on Soviet policy indicates how deep the divisions within the international Marxist camp had become by the late 1960s. Lin was only replying in kind. The intemperance of his attack was typical of the viciousness with which the Soviet Union and the PRC assaulted each other. Informing the insults was a conviction that the others were not merely wrong but were guilty of betrayal. As Communists they had known the truth but had wilfully chosen to reject it. Like lovers who had fallen out of love, they regarded their former partners with a particular hatred and venom. What all this illustrates is that neither the Soviet Union nor the PRC possessed the traditions or political mechanisms for dealing with differences within the Marxist movement. For them, it was all or nothing, wholly right or completely wrong. There was no middle ground, no room for compromise. But was it primarily a dispute over Marxism. You need to estimate what place to give to national rivalry. Russia and China confronted each not only as claimants to the crown of world communism but as two great nations each eager to gain mastery over the other.

Summary Diagram
China and International Revolution

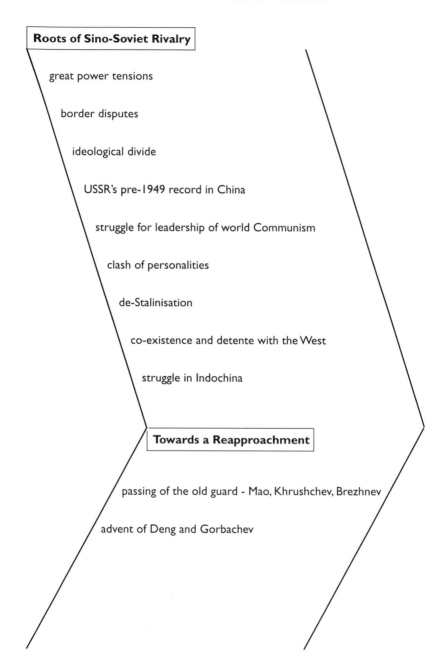

Roots of Sino-Soviet Rivalry

great power tensions

border disputes

ideological divide

USSR's pre-1949 record in China

struggle for leadership of world Communism

clash of personalities

de-Stalinisation

co-existence and detente with the West

struggle in Indochina

Towards a Reapproachment

passing of the old guard - Mao, Khrushchev, Brezhnev

advent of Deng and Gorbachev

7 Conclusion

This chapter sets out to examine the character and pattern of the history of the PRC since 1949. In order to give the necessary perspective to such an assessment, it is helpful to take account of the important developments that occurred in China between the Tiananmen massacre in 1989 and the death of Deng Xiaoping in 1997.

1 China Since Tiananmen

The violent suppression of the Tiananmen protest in June 1989 indicated that China remained a totalitarian state. The post-Mao reforms had not altered this. The CCP retained its absolute authority over the PRC. Immediately after the crushing of the demonstration, Deng Xiaoping and other leaders mounted a public campaign to educate the masses into the 'truth' of what had happened at Tiananmen, explaining how a small group of 'counter-revolutionary elements' had exploited the idealism and naiveté of the students in leading them to challenge the rule of law. In a key speech, which became the official defence of the government's actions, Deng described the student protest as an attempt to destroy all that had been achieved in China since the landmark Third Plenum of the CCP in 1978 had set China on the path to modernisation. He praised the heroic troops of the PLA for yet again acting as the saviours of the Chinese people and mocked those 'comrades who do not understand the nature of the problem':

1 They think it is simply a question of how to treat the masses. Actually, what we face is not simply ordinary people who are unable to distinguish between right and wrong. We also face a rebellious clique and a large number of the dregs of society, who want to topple our country
5 and overthrow our party. Failing to understand this fundamental issue means failing to understand the nature of the incident.
   The incident became very clear as soon as it broke out. They have two main slogans: one is to topple the Communist Party and the other is to overthrow the socialist system. Their goal is to establish a totally
10 Western-dependent bourgeois republic. The people want to combat corruption. This, of course, we accept. We should also take the so-called anti-corruption slogans raised by the people with ulterior motives as good advice and accept them accordingly. But, of course, these slogans are just a front: the heart of these slogans is to topple the Communist
15 Party and overthrow the socialist system.

Yet Deng was very conscious of the basic political problem the CCP faced. If, after forty years of state Communism, China had made no real economic advance, the assumed right of the CCP to govern in perpetuity would become increasingly questionable. If the turmoil of the Great Leap Forward, the Cultural Revolution and the Four

Modernisations in China had all been in vain it would be extremely difficult to sustain the argument that the Party knew what was best for the nation. If China had nothing tangible to show for its efforts, if it remained unable to meet the rising economic aspirations of its people, it would become increasingly difficult to resist the demands for fundamental political change.

Although, as his handling of the Tiananmen protest clearly indicated, Deng could be as ruthless as any of the Party hardliners, he was trying to hold a balance between the Left and Right of the CCP. He was quite clear about what this meant in the Chinese context:

1 In the course of building socialism and trying to modernise we have
   encountered some interference from the 'Left'. We have concentrated
   on combating 'Left' mistakes, because those are the ones we have made
   in the past. But there has also been interference from the Right. What
5 we mean by interference from the Right is the call for total westerniza-
   tion, which would lead not to more advanced socialism but to capitalism.

There was an important ideological aspect to this. The USSR had been condemned in China for its diversion from true Marxism-Leninism. The claim of CCP's political theorists was that China was the genuine interpreter of scientific Socialism. To sustain that belief China had at some point to be able to show practical evidence of the correctness of its claim. Moreover, despite China's traditional isolation it could not wholly ignore the currents running in the wider world. The wholesale collapse of Marxist governments in the Soviet Union and Eastern Europe by the early 1990s suggested that Communism as a political force had been confined to a specific historical period which had now passed. The expected worldwide proletarian revolution had not occurred. Where did that leave Communist China? Was it to maintain its belief that it was a world leader in revolution or was it to withdraw within itself and see its future in traditional terms as a unique culture detached from all others? Deng was certain of one part of the answer; China could not turn its back on the world economically. China's strength, its survival even, depended on its ability to compete in international markets.

The difficulty for Deng Xiaoping and his fellow reformers was that they were encouraging economic reform and opening up to the world commercially while at the same time trying to maintain the status quo politically. This raised another ideological difficulty. The traditional Marxist belief was that distinctions between a nation's economy and its social and political structure were meaningless. Society and politics were simply expressions of the prevailing economic system. When a Communist society's culture was at variance with its proletarian character that culture had to be purged so that it again became the true expression of the people. That had been the justification for the Cultural Revolution. As a pragmatist, Deng might choose to disregard ideology when it suited him but he could not ignore it completely since in the final analysis the right of the CCP to control China rested on an ideology, that of scientific Marxism-Leninism. Deng's abandonment of Maoism had never been intended to imply a weakening in the CCP's belief in its own historical role. The Party under Deng may have appeared to accommodate itself to capitalism on a whole number of points economically, but it had resolutely opposed the extension of political freedoms. Dissidence stood no more chance of being tolerated under Deng than it had under Mao.

Deng had lived through the turmoil and horrors of the anti-Japanese struggle, the civil war between the nationalists and Communists, the Great Leap Forward and the Cultural Revolution. This experience had convinced him that stability was now China's greatest need. He further believed that stability could be achieved only by retaining the socialist system in China. For Deng, socialism was less important as a revolutionary ideology than as a practical system for preserving China from disintegration.

The political rigidity of Deng's outlook was disturbingly illustrated by the statistic that at his death in 1997 there were more political prisoners held in China than there had been in 1976 at the time of Mao's passing. Harry Wu, the noted Chinese dissident, who spent nineteen years as a political prisoner, asserted that in the mid-1990s China was operating a prison-camp system, the 'laogai', larger than the infamous gulag of Stalin's USSR. Wu claimed that the laogai, which was spread throughout China, constituted 'the biggest concentration camp system in human history'.

1 We currently have records of 1,155 camps with between 6 million and 8 million prisoners in them. The world knows that perhaps a few people were killed at Tiananmen Square or directly afterwards during the democracy protests in 1989. I say that incident was peanuts. One way
5 or another, millions of people have been lost in the laogai.

An individual example of the incarcerated millions was Wei Jingshen, one of the first victims in the government's attempt to crush the pro-democracy movement. Wei, who had been sentenced to eighteen years imprisonment in 1979, had his punishment extended by a further fourteen years in 1993 for 'subversion'. His crime was that from prison he had continued to criticise the government for failing to introduce political reforms; in 1989 he had denounced it for its brutality in Tiananmen. Wei had become a hero figure to the pro-democrats, notably so in Hong Kong where thousands marched in protest to demand his release. In the words of Catherine Sampson, *The Observer's* Hong Kong correspondent: 'Wei is the nightmare scenario made flesh, the man who more than anyone else proves Beijing to be incapable of tolerating dissenting views, even if they are peacefully expressed'. Wei was eventually released in 1997. This was not an act of clemency on the part of the Chinese authorities but a ruse to avoid having the ailing Wei die on their hands.

By the mid-1990s the ageing Deng, stricken with Parkinson's disease, had ceased to be actively involved in government. He made his last public appearance in 1994. Yet there is little doubt that he still remained the greatest influence in Chinese affairs. No one was prepared to take the responsibility of altering his policies. Such had been his prominence, having led and reshaped China during the last twenty years of his life, that at his death, aged ninety-two, in 1997, the Western media referred to the passing away of the last emperor. His greatest wish, to live to see the official reincorporation of Hong Kong into China, was denied him by five months. He had believed that China could successfully follow a policy of 'one nation, two systems', that it could modernise its economy and open itself to the outside world while at the same time retaining the absolute authority of the CCP in politics. Time would tell how realistic Deng's hopes had been.

The fundamental problems that Deng Xiaoping's revolution bequeathed to China were perceptively defined by the American analyst, Orville Schell. He suggested that Deng's policies had in effect created 'two separate Chinas that now existed in parallel'.

1 On the one hand there was the new China of entrepreneurs with brief-cases and businessmen with Italian suits; of neon night clubs and five-star hotels; and of Mercedes Benzes equipped with cellular phones. But just behind this impressive facade was the old China of failing state-owned
5 factories filled with angry workers and belching pollution out over the landscape; of poor peasants in poverty-stricken rural areas dreaming of making it in the cities; of prisons where murderers and democracy activists were incarcerated together; of the Red Army whose loyalties were to feudal leaders not to elected officials; and of veteran revolu-
10 tionaries weaned in Marxist-Leninist-Maoist doctrine who could conceive of no path to stability save political repression.

2 The People's Republic of China

In Chapter 1 it was suggested that the history of the PRC can be best understood by reference to its economics, its politics, its ideology and its foreign policy. Let us return to examine those four key areas.

a) Economics

There is no doubting the ambition that underlay the economic policies which China followed under Mao Zedong. He aimed to place the PRC on a par with the world's major industrial powers. But ambition was not enough. His economic strategy proved to be flawed and misconceived. He believed that by relying on China's unlimited manpower he could effect the same advance that the Western industrial nations had made. But Mao lacked the knowledge of agricultural science necessary to understand the reports he received from the countryside. He was also very limited in his understanding of the industrial process. He accepted that industrialisation was essential, but he had a very imperfect idea of what that meant in practice. He simply believed that by a massive deployment of manpower China could achieve the advanced industrialisation it needed. In no sense was Mao qualified as an economic planner. For all his adult life he had been a revolutionary. This is what continued to dominate him and consume his energies. His experience as a political in-fighter and military strategist had in no way prepared him for the task of shaping the economy of a vast nation. His approach was necessarily a series of intuitive leaps. The results were calamitous. His collectivisation programme produced not additional food but famine; his five-year plans wasted rather than successfully exploited China's vast natural and human resources.

Deng Xiaoping tried to pick up the pieces. His four modernisations programme was an attempt to lay an agricultural, industrial and commercial base that would enable China to match the performance of the advanced nations. The method he chose was that of the 'two systems', the adoption of capitalist economics while retaining Communist China's existing political structures. Thus it was that at his death in 1997 Deng left a potentially explosive problem for his successors. How successfully and for how long could the PRC maintain a progressive economic policy that was opening up China to the world with a reactionary political system based on an ideology that the rest of the world had rejected?

b) Politics

In assessing the political record of the PRC it is important to place it in its historical context. Since the fall of the Qings in 1911 the strongest political movements in China have been those which made their priority national regeneration not the extension of political freedoms. The story of the Guomindang in power in the 1930s and 1940s was a clear illustration of this. Chiang Kaishek's overriding concern was the tightening of Nationalist control; the broadening of political and civil rights was not on his agenda. The same centralising of power continued under the Communists after they came to power in 1949. Mao Zedong had two essential aims: to consolidate the CCP's hold over China and to make China safe in a hostile world. At no point did Mao contemplate giving greater personal freedom to the Chinese people.

Western observers often have difficulty in grasping why Communist China was so resolute in its crushing of opposition. But the point to stress is that China has never been democratic. The right of those in authority to the obedience of the people is the traditional basis of

Chinese politics. In 1949 that right, traditionally expressed in the notion of 'the mandate of heaven', had passed to the CCP. It is true that the Communist rulers spoke in terms of proletarian revolution but behind the language of international Marxism they were following a programme that the Qings would have perfectly understood. Their purpose was to bring China into conformity with their own will. It was the duty of the people to follow. The outstanding examples of Mao's application of this doctrine was his launching of the Great Leap Forward and of the Cultural Revolution

Such had been the turmoil created by these policies that Mao's successor, Deng Xiaoping, believed that China's greatest need was a respite from politics. The nation's efforts should be directed to the pursuit of economic growth. Deng redefined the essential purpose of the rule of the CCP as the raising of the living standards of the Chinese people. Yet, even while doing this, Deng reasserted the traditional absolutism of Chinese government. Given China's hierarchic structure, material improvement could be achieved only by direction from the top. Deng asserted that China had no need of further political freedoms. The CCP was sufficient to satisfy all China's wants. That was why he found the pro-democracy movement such an irritant. He believed that it was endangering China's growth by indulging in political fantasies that were both irrelevant and disruptive. China needed not more politics but less. The Revolution had been achieved. The task now for all loyal Chinese was to accept the existing governmental system, which had been fashioned out of the triumphant struggle of the CCP, and under the Party's inspired guidance to work for the economic regeneration of China.

c) Ideology

Historians continue to be divided in their interpretation of the Chinese Revolution that began under Mao Zedong in 1949. Some believe that his successful peasant-based movement introduced a new form of applied Marxism into the world. Others suggest that what characterises Maoism is not its revolutionary credentials but its conformity with Chinese tradition. They argue that behind the Marxist slogans the PRC was engaged in the traditional tasks of consolidating the authority of the central government and of restoring China's superiority over other nations. They also emphasise that Marxism was redrawn to make it fit the Chinese context. Those aspects of it which did not appeal to the Chinese Communists were either jettisoned or modified. A particularly interesting example is that in defining their particular brand of Communism the Chinese spoke of Marxism-Leninism-Maoism. The progression implied in the title was all-important. In Chinese thinking Mao was the greatest of the three interpreters; his wisdom and perception brought to fruition the ideas which Marx and Lenin had struggled to establish. It was as if

Mao Zedong was the last and greatest in a line of prophets.

A critical feature of Maoism was that is was essentially a Chinese, not an international, revolutionary movement. Mao himself was steeped in Chinese history. It was this rather than Marxist theory that guided him in the governing of China. The books which filled his shelves were not Western Marxist texts but the Chinese classics. His favourite was *The General Mirror for the Aid of Government*, an eleventh-century work which surveyed thirteen hundred years of Chinese history and to which he constantly turned for practical guidance. He took his exemplars not from contemporary leaders but from the heroes of China's ancient past. The title often given him in the West of 'the Red Emperor' aptly defines the role which he played in the continuum of Chinese history. China had no tradition of participatory politics. Its people had never developed a concept of citizenship. They had always been subjects in the precise meaning of that term - they were subject to authority. They had no rights; their duty was to obey. The only means by which a tyrannical ruler could be challenged was by rebellion; there was no constitutional process that could be invoked. Rebellions litter the history of China. A few were successful and dynasties changed hands. But, these were more in the way of palace coups than revolutions on a national scale. When there were genuinely popular revolts, as with the Taipings in the nineteenth century, these were crushed with great severity.

Despite its revolutionary appearance, Maoism was never a progressive political ideology. To the great frustration of international Marxists, it remained Chinese and parochial. It is true that Mao regularly acknowledged the great Communist forebears, Marx, Lenin and Stalin, as his inspiration, yet he remained highly selective in his use of their ideas. He never slavishly followed a Marxist orthodoxy and made no effort to apply a systematic Marxist programme in China. He took from Marxism-Leninism those concepts which he judged were relevant to the Chinese situation. Marxism-Leninism was, of course, highly useful in providing the language of revolution. Its critique of Western capitalism was of particular value as an explanation of China's previous subordination to the European imperialists. Its claim to scientific infallibility had an obvious appeal as a justification for the rule of the Chinese Communist Party. An equally attractive Leninist concept was that of democratic centralism; with its emphasis on the Party as the source of truth. This notion slotted perfectly into the traditional pattern of Chinese dictatorial rule.

Yet whenever Mao judged Marxist theory to be inappropriate in the Chinese situation he had no compunction in ignoring it. The most striking example of this was his rewriting of the rules of the dialectic. In strict Marxist ideology, the peasant revolution that Mao had led in China should have been merely the prelude to the proletarian rising of the industrial workers. In defiance of the theory and of the demands from Moscow that he conform to the Soviet interpretation, Mao proceeded as if the success of the peasant movement in China had fulfilled all the requirements of a genuine revolution. This was why he felt no obligation to recognise the Soviet model as superior. It was prior in time but not in importance. It followed from this that China was entitled to assume the leadership of world Communism. This claim was pushed with renewed vigour after the USSR adopted de-Stalinisation, and, in Chinese eyes, corrupted its true socialism by following a policy of liberalisation and of detente with the capitalist West.

Maoism also claimed to lead the anti-colonial struggle, but it was a leadership that required the led to subordinate themselves to Chinese direction. In its dealings with other Marxist movements, the PRC was as insistent as the Soviet Union had been that its particular view of revolution must prevail. Its limited impact on international Marxism is explained by its reluctance to treat other revolutionary parties as equals. China's superior attitude towards foreigners was strikingly similar to that displayed by the emperors in former times. Mao was maintaining a tradition that had deep roots in Chinese history.

Even after the death of Mao Zedong, when his reputation was reassessed and mistakes could at last be attributed to him, it was inconceivable that Deng Xiaoping and the other CCP leaders who had inherited Mao's authority, would make any serious moves to abandon Communism. They had at least to remain formally loyal to the notion of Marxism as the source of political truth. How deeply they still believed in its precepts is difficult to judge, but unless Marxism was upheld their absolute claim to govern China would be undermined. Deng was insistent on this when, during the revolution which bore his name in the 1980s, he was careful to distinguish between political and economic freedoms. He was quite willing to introduce Western-based reforms into the restructuring of the economy but he was adamant that the political system must remain unchanged. He was prepared to contemplate democracy but only in the narrow sense in which he defined it. Democratic centralism would continue to prevail; the CCP already represented the will of the people.

d) Foreign Affairs

Mao Zedong never lost his fear of a Western attack on China. His falling out with the USSR intensified his concern for China's security. The adoption of a crash nuclear programme was one form of response. By the 1960s China had its own atomic and hydrogen weapons. This was a remarkable scientific achievement and appeared to place China in the ranks of the superpowers. Yet, paradoxically, this made China more not less vulnerable since it lacked a weapon-delivery system comparable to those of the West or the USSR. This meant that its threats of nuclear retaliation were largely a matter of bluff. The wisdom of the nuclear programme has also been queried by historians who have pointed out that the amount of effort and capital diverted into it drained vital resources from the Chinese domestic economy at a critical stage in its development.

So long as Mao was in power China's foreign policy was overshadowed by two great rivalries: the Cold War between East and West and the struggle between the USSR and the PRC. But in the period after Mao both these conflicts lessened in intensity until by the 1990s they had ceased altogether. This meant that Deng Xiaoping and his successors, freed from the threat of large-scale military conflict, were able to pursue better relations with the outside world. China did not formally abandon its faith in international revolution but its new stance made it clear that what it wanted with other nations, western and eastern, was not confrontation but trade and commerce. This was what Deng meant by his plan for 'opening China to the world'. The logic of this development appeals to those sinologists who advance the idea that it is unhelpful to view the history of the PRC as a study in applied Communism. They suggest it is more accurate to see the PRC not primarily as a Marxist revolutionary state but as a once-powerful nation trying to regain its place in the world.

3 Western Perceptions of the PRC

Many observers in the Western world tend to await the advent of democracy in China as if this were an inevitable part of its development. This is because the West invariably judges a nation's 'progress' by how near it approaches to the democratic principle. But this is to assess China by alien standards. China is not the West. Its traditions have been fundamentally different. Authoritarianism has been an essential part of its history. It was a far greater crime in Chinese eyes for a dynasty to show weakness than to exercise tyranny. China's greatest problems have occurred when its central government has been weak, as in the last years of the Qing dynasty or in the warlord period in the 1920s. Deng Xiaoping was adamant on this point. Internal stability was China's greatest need. He asserted that to indulge in inappropriate and un-Chinese notions of democracy would be to jeopardise China's hard-won economic gains. Prosperity and growth depended ultimately not on politics but on economics. To pursue the goal of representative government would be to chase shadows. His argument was that China already possessed a genuine representative system. The CCP through its history of struggle had made itself the true voice of the Chinese people. This rendered appeals for greater democracy meaningless.

Understandable Western horror over the Cultural Revolution and the Tiananmen Square massacre has tended to obscure the success of the PRC in achieving political stability and national cohesion. Between the fall of the Manchus in 1911 and the Communists taking power in 1949 China had experienced eight different regimes, none of which had been able to unite the nation or free it from its subjection to the foreigner. In contrast, the PRC under Mao and his successors has regained China's national independence, reclaimed its disputed territories, made itself into a superpower, outlasted the USSR as the only surviving Marxist state of consequence, and developed an economy capable of competing in the world of international commerce. Some would argue that these advances have been bought at the cost of political freedoms. But such an argument would not greatly move the mass of Chinese people who regard the primary duty of their leaders to be the provision of effective government not the spreading of democracy.

Using the Conclusion

This chapter advances a number of propositions:
1. The significance of Chinese history since 1949 is best understood as a continuation of China's 'revolution against the world to join the world', its attempt to achieve modernisation by adopting the progressive features of the Western world while at the same time rejecting the West's decadent social and political values.
2. Maoism was not so much a Marxist ideology as a practical expression of China's age-old belief in its superiority over all other cultures. In the term 'Chinese Communism' it is the adjective not the noun that is important. Mao was engaged in an essentially Chinese exercise. His espousal of worldwide revolution was not an appeal for the unity of international Marxism but a demand that revolutionaries everywhere follow the Maoist path. That is why the USSR became so embittered with the PRC. The Soviet leaders believed that Mao was usurping their place at the head of the international revolutionary movement. But in reality Mao was engaged in a particularly intense form of traditional national self-assertion.
3. Under Mao, who nursed a profound suspicion of all things foreign, China saw itself as beleaguered in a world that was essentially hostile. It was this that gave the air of paranoia about so much of the foreign policy of the PRC and made its relations with the West and the Soviet Union so fraught with misunderstanding.
4. The revolution led by Deng Xiaoping was a remarkable redirection of Chinese affairs, but domestically the new departure was restricted to economic matters. Deng sought better relations with the outside world in order to improve China's commercial prospects. But at home he had no intention of lessening the grip of the CCP on the reins of power or of allowing the development of genuine participatory politics. That, as much as the economic revolution that he inspired, remains his legacy to China.
5. Western views of the PRC have been clouded by a failure to appreciate the character of Chinese history and a reluctance to judge China by its own standards. This means that the very considerable

achievements of the PRC in sustaining itself over half a century tend to be overlooked.

It is important that you test these arguments for yourself by referring to the relevant chapters in this book and by comparing them with the ideas contained in as many as possible of the texts listed in the further reading section. That way you will reach your own independent conclusions, supported by evidence, about the main issues discussed in this book.

Chronological Table

1949	PRC established
1950	Tibet invaded by PLA
	Mao paid official visit to USSR
	Sino-Soviet Treaty signed
	USA committed itself to protection of Taiwan
1950-53	Korean War
1951	'Anti-movements' launched
1952-56	China's first Five-Year Plan
1952	Political parties other than CCP banned
1953	Construction of Third Line began
	Death of Stalin in USSR
1955	PRC attended Bandung Conference of non-aligned nations
1956	Khrushchev began de-Stalinisation programme
	Hungarian Rising crushed by Soviet forces
1957	Hundred Flowers Campaign launched
	Mao attended Marxist convention in Moscow
1958-62	The Great Leap Forward
1958-61	Widespread famine in China
1958	Khrushchev visited China
	Mao Zedong gave up Presidency of PRC
	Matsu and Qemoy shelled by PLA
	Lin Biao became Minister of Defence
	Great Leap Forward criticised by Soviet Union
1961	Chinese delegation walked out of CPSU Congress in Moscow
1962	Liu Shaoqi and Deng Xiaoping appointed to tackle the famine
	Sino-Indian border war broke out
	PRC condemned Soviet policy in Cuba
1963	Mao's Little Red Book became a standard Chinese text
	The Diary of Lei Feng published
1964	A-bomb exploded by Chinese
1965	*The Dismissal of Hai Rai from Office* attacked by Maoists
1966	Mao reappeared in public
	Liu and Deng dismissed
1966-76	The Great Proletarian Cultural Revolution
1967	H-bomb exploded by Chinese
1969	USSR attempted to outlaw China from international Communism
	PRC and USSR threatened each other with rocket attacks
1971	Sino-American talks began
	USA accepted PRC's right to represent China at UN
	Lin Biao killed in plane crash
1972	President Nixon visited China
	'Criticise Lin Biao and Confucius' campaign started

1973	Liu Shaoqi died in prison
	Deng Xiaoping returned to government
1975	Death of Chiang Kaishek
	PRC backed Pol Pot in Cambodia
1976	Death of Zhou Enlai
	Tiananmen Incident in Beijing
	Tangshan earthquake
	Death of Mao Zedong
	Hua Guofeng became CCP Chairman
	Gang of Four arrested
1977	Deng regained position as CCP Secretary
1978	Third Plenun convened
	Four Modernisations adopted
1979	Pro-democracy movement began
	Wei Jingsheng imprisoned
	Full diplomatic relations established between PRC and USA
1980	Gang of Four put on trial
1981	PRC issued Nine Principles on Taiwan
1982	Margaret Thatcher visited China for talks on Hong Kong
1984	Sino-British Joint Declaration on Hong Kong
1986	Protests occurred in China's leading universities
1988	Chinese sank Vietnamese warships in Spratly Islands dispute
1989	Death of Hu Yaobang
	Mikhail Gorbachev visited China
	Pro-democracy demonstration crushed in Beijing
1992	USA conferred 'most favoured nation' status on PRC
1997	Death of Deng Xiaoping
	Hong Kong returned to China

Glossary

Chinese names in their Pinyin and Wade-Giles forms

Pinyin	Wad-Giles
Anhui	Anhwei
Beijing	Peking
Bo Yibo	Po Yipo
Chen Boda	Chen Po-ta
Chen Duxui	Chen Tu-hsiu
Chongqing	Chungking
Daxing	Tsa-hsing
Deng Xiaoping	Teng Hsiao-ping
Duan Qirui	Tuan Chi-jui
Fang Lizhi	Fang Li-chih
Feng Yuxiang	Feng Yu-hsiang
Fuzhou	Foochow
Fujian	Fukien
Gao Gang	Kao Kang
Gansu	Kansu
Guangzhou	Canton
Guandong	Kwangtung
Guangxu	Kuang Hsu
Guangxi	Kwangsi
Guishou	Kweichow
Guomingdang	Kuomintang
Hangzhou	Hangchow
Henan	Honan
Heilongjang	Heilunkiang
Hebei	Hopei
Hefei	Hofei
Hua Guofeng	Hua Kuopfeng
Hubei	Hupei
Hu Yaobang	Hu Yao-pang
Jiang Jieshi	Chiang Kai-shek
Jiang Jingguo	Chiang Ching-kuo
Jiang Qing	Chiang Ching
Jiang Wun	Chiang Wun
Jiangxi	Kiansi
Lin Biao	Lin Piao
Liu Shaoqi	Liu Shao-chi
Mao Zedong	Mao Tse-tung
Mao Yuanxin	Mao Yuan-hsin
Nanjing	Nanking
Peng Dehuai	Peng Teh-huai
Peng Zhen	Peng Chen

Quemoy	Jinmen
Qin Shi Huang	Shi Huang-ti
Qinghai	Tsinghai
Rao Rashi	Jao Shu-shi
Shaanxi	Shensi
Shandong	Shantung
Shantou	Swatow
Shanxi	Shansi
Sun Yatsen	Sun Yat-sen
Sichuan	Szechwan
Taiwan	Formosa
Wang Dengxing	Wang Tung-hsing
Wang Hongwen	Wang Hung-wen
Wang Jingwei	Wang Ching-wei
Wang Jinxi	Wang Ching-hsi
Wuhan	Wuchang
Xian	Sian
Xiamen	Amoy
Xiefuzhi	Hsieh Fu-chih
Xinhua	Hsinhua
Xinjiang	Sinkiang
Xizang	Hsi-tsang
Xu Shiyou	Hsu Shih-yu
Yanan	Yenan
Yangzi	Yangtze
Yan Jioqi	Yan Chao-chi
Yan Xishan	Yen Hsi-shan
Yao Wenyuan	Yao Wen-yuan
Ye Jianying	Yeh Chien-ying
Zhang Chunqiao	Chang Chun-chiao
Zhao Ziyang	Chao Tzu-yang
Zhuhai	Chuhai
Zhou Enlai	Chou En-lai
Zhu De	Chuh The
Zunyi	Tsunyi

Further Reading

The following is a selective list of the many studies of Communist China since 1949, which are written in English or are available in English translation. Where possible, reference is to the latest paperback edition.

1 General Surveys

The standard reference book on China in this period is *The Cambridge History of China* vols 14 and 15, edited by **Roderick MacFarquar** and **John K. Fairbank** (CUP, 1987-91). Among the contributors to it are many of the chief authorities on modern Chinese history. Undoubtedly, the outstanding text on modern China is **Jonathan Spence's** *The Search for Modern China* (W.W. Norton, 1990). Another important book by this prolific British scholar is *The Gate of Heavenly Peace: the Chinese and their Revolution 1895-1980* (Faber and Faber, 1982), which describes the history of the period from the viewpoint of lesser-known figures in Chinese public life. Also highly recommended is **Spence's** collaboration with **Annping Chin**, *The Chinese Century: A Photographic History* (HarperCollins, 1996); this combines superb illustrations with a masterly commentary. A lively and comprehensive overview of modern China is to be found in **Dick Wilson**, *China: the Big Tiger* (Little Brown, 1996) and in **John Gittings**, *Real China: from Cannibalism to Karaoke*, (Simon & Schuster, 1996). A particularly clear treatment of politics in Mao's China is provided by **Richard C. Thornton's** *China: a Political History 1917-80* (Westview Press, 1982) while an interesting perspective is provided by the Hong-Kong Chinese historian, **W.S.K. Waung**, in his *Revolution and Liberation: A Short History of Modern China 1900-1970* (Heinemann, 1971). A very useful short introduction, containing a full list of modern works, is **P.J. Bailey's** *China in the Twentieth Century* (Basil Blackwell, 1988). Other broad surveys of particular value are **S.A.M. Adshead**, *China in World History* (Macmillan, 1995) and **John King Fairbank**, *China: A New History* (Belknap Press, 1992); the latter has an excellent bibliography. Also to be recommended are **Henry McAleavy**, *The Modern History of China* (Weidenfeld and Nicolson, 1967), and **Peter M. Mitchell**, *China: Tradition and Revolution* (Edward Arnold, 1977), which offer lively accounts of the Maoist years. **Immanuel C.Y. Hsu** in *The Rise of Modern China*, (New York, 1983) deals with the political struggles of that period. **Hsu** has also edited an interesting set of interpretations under the title *Readings in Modern Chinese History* (Oxford, 1971). **Dun J. Li**, *The Road to Communism: China Since 1912* (Van Nostrand, 1969) contains a wide range of illuminating sources, linked by an informed commentary. **F. Schurmann** and **O. Schell** have edited sets of very useful source material in their *Communist China* (Penguin, 1974).

2 Particular Themes

Mao Zedong's government of China after 1949 is covered in detail in **Roderick MacFarquar's** *The Origins of the Cultural Revolution* (Columbia UP, 1983) and in his *From the Hundred Flowers to the Great Leap* (Harvard UP, 1989). The famine that resulted from Mao's Great Leap Forward and the West's reluctance to acknowledge it is chillingly described in **Jasper Becker's** *Hungry Ghosts: China's Secret Famine* (John Murray, 1996). Of the many studies of the Cultural Revolution to be recommended are **Lynn White**, *Politics of Chaos* (Princeton UP, 1989), **Anita Chan**, *Children of Mao* (University of Washington Press, 1985), and **Chihua Wen**, *The Red Mirror* (Plymbridge, 1996). The views of the former Red Guards and their victims are to be found in **Gao Yuan**, *Born Red: a Chronicle of the Cultural Revolution* (Stanford UP, 1987) and **Nien Cheng**, *Life and Death in Shanghai* (Grove, 1986). The Deng Revolution is analysed in **Richard Baum**, ed., *China's Four Modernisations* (Columbia, 1980). The pro-democracy movement that led up to Tiananmen Square is the subject of **David Bachman's** and **Dali L.Yang's** *China's Struggle for Democracy* (Sharpe, 1991). The Tiananmen massacre itself is can be studied from two opposing stances. **Jiang Zhifen's** *Countdown to Tiananmen* (Harvester, 1990) gives the demonstrators' side of things while the government's view is provided by **Che Muqi's** *Beijing Turmoil: More than Meets the Eye* (Beijing Foreign Languages Press, 1992). Deng Xiaoping's legacy to China is provocatively covered from a Western viewpoint in **Orville Schell's**, *Mandate of Heaven* (Warner Books, 1995). Illuminating studies of the PRC's foreign policy are contained in **Bruce Cummings**, *The Origins of the Korean War* (Princeton UP, 1990), **Herbert J.Ellison**, ed., *The Sino-Soviet Conflict* (University of Washington Press, 1982), **Gordon H.Chang**, *The United States, China and the Soviet Union, 1948-72* (Stanford UP, 1990) and **Samuel S. Kim**, *The Third World in Chinese World Policy* (Princeton UP, 1989). The anti-Stalinist but pro-Soviet Russian writer, **Roy Medvedev** offers an absorbing view of Chinese attitudes to the outside world in his *China and the Superpowers* (Blackwell, 1986). Two American scholars, **Andrew J. Nathan** and **Robert S. Ross**, have written a stimulating analysis of the PRC's foreign policy from the perspective of China's search for security in a hostile world, *The Great Wall and the Empty Fortress* (W.W. Norton, 1997). The growth of Taiwan receives a scholarly treatment in **John Cooper's** *A Quiet Revolution: Political Development in the Republic of China* (Washington, 1988). China's suppression of Tibet as experienced by the victims is movingly described by **Palden Gyatso** in his *Fire Under the Snow* (Harvill, 1997). Of the many books that have now appeared in English detailing the persecution of political dissidents within the PRC perhaps the most authoritative are **Harry Wu's** *Laogai - China's Gulag* (Chatto & Windus, 1993) and **Zhang Xianliang's** *My Bodhi tree* (Secker, 1996). Economic developments in the PRC are clearly and perceptively covered in **David J. Pyle's** *China's Economy, 1949-94 From Revolution to Reform* (Macmillan, 1997) while *China's Modern Economy in Historical Perspective* edited by **Dwight Perkins** (Stanford University Press, 1975) is an important collection of essays on China's economic relations with the West.

3 Biographies

The first authoritative biography of Mao to appear in English was **Stuart Schram's** *Mao Tse-Tung* (Penguin, 1975). Also valuable is the same author's *Mao Tse-Tung Unrehearsed, Talks and letters: 1956-71* (Penguin, 1975). Another highly regarded study is **Jerome Ch'en's** *Mao and the Chinese Revolution* (Oxford University Press, 1965). An idiosyncratic but highly readable treatment of Mao is by the American traveller and journalist, **Harrison E. Salisbury**, *The New Emperors Mao and Deng: A Dual Biography* (Harper Collins, 1993). A particularly notable biography, based on the recollections of one of Mao's body-guards, is **Quan Yanchi's** *Mao Zedong: Man Not God* (Foreign Languages Press Beijing 1992). As its title suggests, it offers a balanced appraisal, something unknown in China before the 1980s when only hagiography was permitted. Among those books which adopt a strongly critical stance towards the role of Mao and the CCP in repub-lican China are **Siao Yu's** *Mao and I Were Beggars* (Syracuse University, 1959). **Wang Ming's** *Mao Tse-tung* (Moscow, 1975) is a rare example of a pro-Soviet, anti-Maoist Chinese writer. A brief but useful survey of the main features of Mao's career is to be found in **Delia Davin's** *Mao Zedong* (Sutton, 1997). Extracts from Mao Zedong's major works, accompanied by an informed introduction to his career are to be found in **Ann Freemantle**, *Mao Tse-tung* (Mentor, 1971). Students are encouraged to dip into *Quotations from Chairman Mao Tse-tung* (Foreign Languages Pres Beijing, 1966), 'the Little Red Book' which became the bible of China in the 1960s. Particularly valuable insights into Mao's character, medical history and behaviour are provided by his doctor, **Li Zhisiu**, in *The Private Life of Chairman Mao* (Chatto and Windus, 1994). In addition to **Harrison Salisbury's** *The New Emperors*, interesting studies of Deng Xiaoping are **Richard Evans's** *Deng Xiaoping and the Making of Modern China* (OUP, 1991)and **David Goodman's** *Deng Xiaoping* (Cardinal, 1990). The most accessible collection of Deng's writings are in **Deng Xiaoping** *Fundamental Issues in Present-Day China* (Foreign Languages Press, 1987). Worthwhile studies of Taiwan's leader, Chiang Kaishek, are **Emily Hahn's** *Chiang Kai-shek, an Unauthorised Biography* (New York, 1955) which paints him in a favourable light and the more critical analysis by **Louise Strong**, *China Fights for Freedom* (New World Press, 1963).

Index